Top Sellers Tell…

Top Sellers Tell...

Moehr & Associates

iUniverse, Inc.
New York Lincoln Shanghai

Top Sellers Tell...

iUniverse books may be ordered through booksellers or by contacting:

iUniverse
2021 Pine Lake Road, Suite 100
Lincoln, NE 68512
www.iuniverse.com
1-800-Authors (1-800-288-4677)

ISBN-13: 978-0-595-38644-4 (pbk)
ISBN-13: 978-0-595-83025-1 (ebk)
ISBN-10: 0-595-38644-X (pbk)
ISBN-10: 0-595-83025-0 (ebk)

Printed in the United States of America

Publisher: Moehr & Associates
President: Karen R. Moehr

Moehr & Associates is a marketing and consulting company specializing in assisting direct sales professionals, small and home-based businesses in growing and prospering.

Direct Seller Guide: Get Booked Solid!, *Direct Seller's Boot Camp Blast, PUMP Marketing News Guides and Direct Sales Business Blaster* are property of Moehr & Associates.

The participants and their interviews were obtained to help guide and mentor direct sales professionals. They were not remunerated for their participation. The information given in the interviews is included as it was submitted to us with only minor editing. The author and publisher of this book shall be held harmless from any responsibility due to misrepresentation or inaccuracies of the participants and their interviews.

Top Sellers Tell...

Top Direct Sales Professionals Tell How They Achieved Big Success

- Growing your business
- Mistakes they've made along the way
- What they have learned
- Advice on building and managing a team
- Top tips for sales, booking, recruiting and inventory
- How to stay motivated
- Suggestions for profitable sales parties
- What you must do to have a thriving career
- How they achieved big success!

Moehr & Associates

Creators of:

- The Direct Seller's Guide: Get Booked Solid!
- PUMP Direct Sales News Guide
- The Direct Seller's Boot Camp Blast
- Direct Sales Business Blaster

"This is a fascinating and helpful book!"

Acknowledgements

To you, the direct sales professional, who strives, perseveres and thrives in the face of disappointment, frustration and challenge.

We are thankful for the contributors who generously took their time to submit their interviews, re-submit and then wait in the face of delays in getting this book finished. They are each special and appreciated not only by their ever-growing teams, but by our small team of marketing and publishing specialists.

In addition, we would like to thank our contributing interviewers who helped obtain some of the interviews that are included in this book: Marcia Schutte, John Fuhrman and Todra Payne.

Finally, personally, I must give special thanks to my family: Rodger, my never-ending source for strength, courage, and love as well as a fountain of business knowledge; Bella Boo, my little ray of light from whom I get the ability to approach each day with more fun and continuous wonder, and to Keek, my buddy through thick and thin.

Note:

The sales professionals who have participated in this book were chosen at random. They were not compensated for their participation. They have offered their interviews and accompanying data for the sole purpose of offering information to the reader. Claims of team numbers, sales/financial figures and achievements have been included exactly as reported by the sales professional. The author, Moehr & Associates, makes no affirmation of fact of any of the information given by the participants.

Contents

Preface

As marketing consultants who counsel many direct sales professionals over the course of a year, we speak to lots of new reps who are just trying to get their business off the ground. We offer many publications and programs to help these consultants market and grow their businesses. We truly understand the equal parts of frustration determination that developing a new business can foster. We have dedicated the last few years of our marketing business to helping the direct sales professional find inspiration, new ideas, unique tips, and stellar service programs to set them apart from their competition.

We also speak to a significant number of seasoned pros who have large teams and still seek new information to continue to grow their businesses. As such, we have learned that the bottom line is that whether new or seasoned, the search for motivation, new ideas and unique tips is what drives the dedicated professional to keep growing. It is also what keeps us looking for new and innovative ways to service that industry.

When planning to publish this book, the objective was clear: We wanted to offer insightful and helpful interviews detailing what some of the top sellers in the direct sales industry have learned during the course of building their business. It needn't contain 100 interviews for the reader to understand the common factor for success. The interviewees included in this book have generously opened up and spoken candidly (some more than others) about their experiences in working in direct sales and running their own business.

This book offers the opportunity to learn from some of the most dedicated, motivated, and success-oriented sellers in the business. What is gleaned will be individual. What worked for one seller may be contradicted by another, depending upon the difference of their products or experiences. What one seller's needs may be, another may need something completely different. It will be up to the reader to understand that these sellers have accomplished success by learning what worked for them and by duplicating that system again and again.

It is with our sincere appreciation to the participating sellers that we can offer this book to readers with a dream of success in their heart. These sellers were not paid, however they each share similar traits essential for direct sales success: A strength to persevere and burning desire to grow their business. They are inspirational business leaders that enjoy mentoring others to triumph. This is precisely one reason they are the ones we aspire to emulate. They care enough to show others the ropes they've climbed to reach their goals. They have shared their victories, their mistakes and their unique recipes for success. To them we say thank you.

Introduction

Wow. The publication of this book took several months, lengthy delays, lots of emails and faxes and all the while we held the constant belief that it could indeed be helpful to those for whom it was written. Compiling interviews and updating them wasn't difficult. Many top sales professionals were eager to provide candid and helpful information to help others grow. While all the interviews are undeniably interesting and useful, you may find some are more forthcoming than others.

All who participated in this project are arguably hard-working team leaders and sales professionals. A few, in particular, seem to stand out as stellar leaders. They give the extra little bit that really creates a helpful and interesting interview. Or perhaps they just enjoyed this process more than others. Whatever the reason, you'll find each leader has his or her own style and own way of getting their points across. While you may enjoy one interview more than another, they are each a solid source of helpful information.

As these sellers endured a wait of nearly a year (some more) to see their words in print, they all shared several indisputable traits: The ability to persevere, lend a hand and stay positive. As you read through the interviews you will notice some answers are decidedly contradictory. However you will also notice there are common threads woven through the pages. These are the people that don't make excuses, don't wait for the perfect time to "just get it done" and don't let the little things defeat them.

Without exception, they each urge persistence and enthusiasm. It's understood that these are the traits that top salespeople and leaders need to attain the top levels. However, hearing it from the proverbial horses' mouths gives credence to the concepts and makes them seem all that more important. Those are the qualities that have seen them through the mistakes, learning experiences and challenges.

Not a revelation or magic formula, they are just expressions of good old fashioned hard work.

While reading this book, you'll hopefully come across a few ideas that will "click" with you. We recommend you highlight these or jot them down in the "Notes" pages included in this book. It will probably be helpful to read through it a couple of times.

If you have the dream of building an enormous team or just developing a small but solid business for years to come, the advice, tips, and experience of these sellers is something to heed. While one style may work better for you than another, the proven successful knowledge of these sellers is hard to ignore. To be one of the best, you must look to many resources to stay motivated, keep learning and increase your own knowledge base. Hopefully this book will be one that gives you that inner spark and a point of reference whenever you start to wonder "How did they do it?" and more importantly "How can I do it too?"

Direct Sales:
A Powerful Career Choice

Direct sales: It's perennial industry that has grown even more in recent years. Why is it so popular? The idea of working from home, selling products that you love, building a team and achieving top level salaries, prizes and recognition is a provocative idea and proven career. It sounds marvelous and to see what some of the top earners of the industry make, it can be a lucrative and enjoyable business for years and years. However, with so much to offer, with such go-at-your-own-pace directives and with the opportunity to build a business doing something you really love, why do some not succeed? Why do hopeful recruits sign on the dotted line to join their company of choice only to drop out a year, or a few months later?

It isn't lack of support. Direct sales offers one of the most supportive environments of any business venture. With team meetings, corporate events, and a plethora of motivational literature, it should be fairly easy to stay interested. It offers the ability to work your own schedule, grow as little or as much as you like and essentially, write your own ticket. If you decide to build a team, it offers an opportunity to make a substantial income without even working a traditional full-time schedule. However, as wonderful as the career can be, it can also be rife with disappointment, difficulties and frustration for those who are unprepared or uneducated in the particular skills required to run a business.

Why the Trouble?

What is it about direct sales that it results in failure for some and prosperity for others? The key to this is something you'll find, in one shape or form, in every one of our seller's stories: The desire to succeed by doing what it takes. That's it. It isn't that one seller sells well and another recruits well. It isn't that one seller uses advertising successfully while another thinks it's a waste of money. It isn't because one seller carries inventory and another believes inventory isn't necessary. The common threads are determination, persistence, and the ability to get past the daily difficulties to stay motivated and keep moving forward.

You've heard it before. You know you must persist and work hard. You know you need to stay energized and work your plan. You've read the books and listened to the tapes to stay motivated and learn. You've heard top sellers say "Just pick up the phone and make 100 phone calls a day for success!" Oh really? Well, of course in the numbers game of sales that will probably work, but will you actually do it? And if it isn't something that you will actually do, then how helpful is it? Picking up the phone and calling 100 people may be a ridiculously difficult task for some people while others have no problem with it whatsoever.

Most people who get involved in direct sales understand that it is sales they are signing up to be involved with, but many of them would rather be called just about anything other than salesperson. The term sales is scary to some, which may account for the popular term "sharing" that many direct sales companies urge their consultants to insert in their mental career image. This helps them get past the idea that they are selling. It's a friendlier term. They are simply sharing what they've found with others.

Sales: From Secret to Sensational.

It's pretty simple. It isn't wrong or illegal or even unpleasant, but some reps who work in direct sales just cannot seem to get past the idea that they are just that…in a sales position. They may not want to call themselves a direct sales representative. The industry often uses the term "consultant" or some other non-sales title.

Whatever you call it, direct sales ultimately rests in the ability to get a product to another for money.

However, any mental block a person may have regarding sales can change rather quickly. When the sales and re-orders pour in, the term "sales" may become less scary and even enjoyable to anyone who may have been uneasy with the title. A party with $500.00 in sales can leave a rep driving home with a smile on her face. A $75.00 sales re-order will elicit a sincere happiness in her chosen profession. It doesn't take much to get past the off-putting image a new rep may have had of sales. It just takes a few solid sales and the ability to get more. The profit can also be quite impressive. The figures can start adding up allowing for a rep to proudly assert "I'm a direct sales professional and it's a great job!" It can be a sensational feeling when you finally understand the power of this career.

If a few strong sales are all it takes to get a rep from start to successful, then what's so tough? The problem seems to lie in not getting some initial sales, but in keeping that momentum going. Initially, a rep is excited and tells everyone about her new business. She shares how much she enjoys the products and usually a friend or relative will have a show or party to get her started. If the rep is motivated and courageous, she books more from that party. This will ensure she has another sales event in which to profit and build her business. However, if she is afraid to ask or doesn't show the party guests and the hostess how advantageous having a show can be (free gifts, special treatment, etc.), she will likely go home wondering how in the world she's going to get this business going. This is the thought process that leads to drop outs.

The sellers in this book obviously had a similar thought or two early in their career. They persisted on to find their own way to make it in this business. As you make your way through this book, you'll obviously see some characteristics you share with these sellers. You'll identify with some more than others. Hopefully you will understand that while they've taken the steps to act and follow through on the traits that made them successful, these traits are not that unique. They run in varying degrees in nearly everyone. It's just a matter of refining, finding systems that work, and powering forward to get what you want.

The Power of Systems

Direct sales companies are famous for using the basic sales principle of contacting your "circle of influence." This is whomever you know: friends, relatives, work associates, your kids' teachers, your church group, your yoga class members, etc. This isn't a bad idea and it does work. However, when your circle grows tired of hearing about your company, where do you turn for new leads and new prospects? This is where learning from others who have faced the same dilemma can be helpful. Your team leaders and upline members can be of enormous help, however they can be busy and difficult to pin down for all of the questions you may have.

Our sellers have faced this problem, and many others, to become some of the more successful members in their particular companies. They have learned what works for them. They have developed a proven, workable system for their business. Along the way, they've wasted money, time and effort doing what hasn't worked to get to where they are today. What you'll find is that there isn't one road to success. What works for you may not work for your very best friend in the same exact business. It isn't a one-size-fits-all recipe. Depending upon what your particular needs are, you may find one seller's tips to be a perfect fit while another's wouldn't work for you.

To get your own unique success formula, you have to have spent some time in your business. You have to get over some road bumps and experience some successes. The system that works for you will become apparent soon enough. As soon as it does, you need to put a plan in place to duplicate it again and again. The concept of a system is a powerful force for your business. It will let you know what will bring you profit, and what will lose you money. It will let you know how and who to recruit and when to let go. It will give you insight into building a strong, profitable team. In the meantime, you have our successful sellers to turn to in order to help you start developing your own system!

As you start to recognize and work your own success system, you will gain more courage, confidence, and the accompanying profits and growth.

The "system" is a term you can learn a lot about by reading nearly any sales guru's analysis of how to build a business. It is a proven step-by-step action that results in your desired outcome. You can build systems for recruiting, for booking, for selling, for motivating and managing, for administrative work, etc. You probably already have several systems in place right now. For instance, if you know you like to put your bills in a certain file and then pay them all on the first and 15th day of the month; that is a system that works for you for getting your bills paid. You likely don't deviate from it very often since it works and gives you the desired outcome: Your bills get paid on time.

You can develop the same type of simple system for building every aspect of your business, like booking sales parties. Once you find a way that works and you can often book parties from it, repeat it again and again and again. Why re-invent the wheel? You can tweak it and update it as times and your needs change, but it will always be your proven system for getting bookings.

The great thing about systems is that they are able to be duplicated and taught. Once you build your team, you can share your system with your recruits. You can make it easier for them to succeed, at least in some areas, so they won't become discouraged and drop out. As they develop their own systems, they can change what they need to make them work for them. And so it goes to create a strong team, which as you probably already know, is the foundation for developing a profitable, long-term direct sales business.

Joining: Just the First Step

You find a company you really like. You use the products and enjoy them so much you feel you could easily sell them. You make the decision and sign up. You get your kit. You use your products, learn about them, and start to understand the benefits of each one. You are ready to get rolling. You are ready to (gasp) start selling. You get your best friend to hold a party. Then a co-worker at your office has one for you. You manage to hold a fairly decent open house and invite all your neighbors. You are seeing some sales and maybe even the very start of your own team. Then what? Your calendar is wide open and you don't have another party planned or even on the horizon. What next?

> *When I signed up with my company, my Director was really nice. She had me over for some training meetings and I was really excited at first. But I had just moved to town and when I talked to her about how to get bookings, she just gave me the typical print-out from the company about talking to your "circle of influence." It wasn't any help since my circle was over thousand miles away in my hometown!*

This story isn't unusual. While some recruiters are immensely talented at training and mentoring their team, others just don't seem to be able to address their individual team members' problems. They may rely too heavily on what worked for them, or what the company suggests. Each individual member of your team will have different needs and different difficulties. Identifying them and doing the work necessary to help them overcome their stumbling blocks will pay off in keeping a strong, motivated team working for you for years.

If you are new to running your own business and working from home you may possibly require a little more assistance than "just contact everyone you know." The information included in these interviews and by talking to other top sellers can help you open the door to new ideas and what has been proven to work. If you are naturally outgoing and have no problem walking up to people and introducing yourself and your products, that's wonderful. Congratulations. We mean that from the bottom of our heart. You are lucky. Many of us would rather chew off our own arm than walk up to a total stranger and introduce ourselves, much less start talking about our business in hopes of getting a new booking or customer. Yet we desire the success we see others achieving in this field. There must be another way.

Of course, telling everyone you know about your business in the beginning can get you off to a wondrous start, but you will need a plan to continue the momentum. You may look at advertising, joining local leads groups, the internet, and more. You may wonder if they work. Should you spend the time? Should you invest the money? Many times, it's just trial and error that teaches you what you want to know. However, by learning from others what their experiences have been, you can start further down the road than point A. This can save you money, disappointment, and frustration.

Finding a system that works for you and developing the confidence to continue working on your business are two of the most important building blocks you'll uncover as you proceed. Learning what brings profits, recruits, and referrals is a road many like you have traveled before. Although you may feel like it at times, rest assured, you are not alone.

This book should help you realize that the road bumps you are experiencing while trying to build your business have been navigated before. These sellers' stories, advice, and tips will help you understand that your dream for a successful business can come true. What they have in common are not superhuman qualities, just the ability to persevere, learn what works for them and do it over and over again, and be patient. They know success doesn't happen overnight. They share those traits and the enviable confidence and courage to do what it takes. If you think you have these qualities, as you read through their interviews you will probably find yourself thinking "If they did it, so can I!"

❤

Interview:

Phyllis Luther

Company: Jafra Cosmetics International
Title: District Director II
Where: Murrysville, PA

Phyllis is an outgoing and experienced direct sales authority. She's truly a professional who cares about the consultants and managers in her team. Phyllis maintains excellent communication and you get the sense that she is one organized and efficient business professional. Take a look at her team numbers and amazing longevity to understand that Phyllis truly "walks her talk."

How long have you been with your company?
I started with Jafra in 1979.

How long have you been at your present level?
Since 1990

How large is your sales team?
Total: Direct Consultants and Indirect Consultants: 800+; Direct Managers: 7; Indirect Managers: 12

Tell us about yourself
I have been married for 28 years. We have one son, Christopher, who is 26 years old. Formerly, I was a Research Analyst for a heart pacemaker company with a degree in Consumer Services & Business. I once weighed 100 pounds more than

I do now and 19 years ago I lost the weight (100 pounds), so my most important hobby is to continue to watch my diet and to work out so I have kept the weight off.

Briefly describe your company (objective, services, products, etc.)

Jafra specializes in cutting-edge skin care, plus a complete product line with color, nail, spa, fragrances, men's products, full body care, and more.

What do you like best about your job?

The flexibility and knowing that I can work the way I choose. I am the one to dictate this, not someone else. I can choose to work as hard as I want and either increase or decrease my pace at any time. In addition, I really enjoy seeing the success of women in this company and also mentoring so many women who build and grow in this program.

Have you worked with any other direct sales companies?

No.

What principles have you followed to reach your current position with the company?

Overall, I try to practice the "STP" method of working: See The People, Set The Pace, Sell The Product, See The Potential, Share The Program, and See The Profit!

Also I:

1. Hold 3–4 Pampering Parties/Sessions per week.
2. Bring a consultant to train at each of my Pampering Sessions.
3. Focus on my strengths.
4. Enjoy the process. My enjoyment will attract others to do what I do.

What mistakes have you made?

So many! But this is what makes me a good mentor. I experience what my consultants do. It is truly the *Feel, Felt, Found* method because I have experienced 99% of every problem or mistake that they will encounter. I've found that I also continue to discover that I want success for someone more than they want it for themselves, which can be a good thing because it's my belief in them, but I need to also know when to let them go.

In your opinion, what does it really take to achieve your level of success?

1. Daily disciplines make the difference. Don't procrastinate over doing what is necessary. So many times we think more about what we have to do than to just do it and get it done. Hire an assistant to do what is necessary, but that doesn't need your personal touch. I began with hiring a high school girl to do necessary tasks such as stamping brochures, labeling products, and some computer tasks. I still have a part-time assistant who does this, plus additional duties which frees me up to do the work that only I can do.

2. Learn to go with the flow. Every day is different and in a people business, it is so important to realize that the phone can ring, urgent emails can be received, the UPS truck that should deliver your order doesn't arrive or you only receive a partial shipment, etc. and the whole day can be changed in an instant.

3. During adversity, keep focus on your dream and realize that if you keep doing the "building" things rather than the "busy" things, everything will work out; maybe not on your time schedule or the necessary deadline, but when it does happen, it usually feels just as good!

What are your top sales tips?

1. Hold 3–4 parties every week.

2. Follow through within 48 hours on potential bookings and potential recruits.

3. Truly "master" your set presentation and booking talk.

What are your top recruiting tips? What helps you recruit?

1. Keep your job simple and fun and able to be duplicated.

2. Do a 10-minute "Recruiting Game" at every party: Spend three minutes on your "I story" and seven minutes where guests ask questions (but only about your job as a consultant) and they receive tickets for each question. Whoever has the most tickets after 5–7 minutes receives a prize.

What have you earned at the company (trips, cars, prizes, etc.)

I've earned trips, my ultimate turn-on! I've earned many to Europe: Spain, Greece, France, Italy, etc. Also, I've earned trips to Hawaii and most of the exciting areas of the U.S.: Arizona, Florida, New Orleans, New York, etc.

I've also earned cars and car programs, which award cash so you can choose your own car. Plus, I've earned many prizes of just about everything, including china, crystal, silverware, appliances, stereos, etc.

What words of advice can you give to a consultant who really wants to grow their business?

Spend 50% of your time on building your own personal business and the other 50% on recruiting or sponsoring others. This way you have your "checking account" per se—instant profit when you sell the products and a "saving's account" which is your future paycheck when you invest in and train others to be successful.

What do you want to achieve next?

To increase team recruiting and promoting more managers. Also, to continue as number one in the company for personal sales (as I have been for the last 23 years).

What do you enjoy most: Recruiting or sales? Why?

I enjoy different aspects of both. Sales can be similar to a checking account. There is immediate income and the instant high of meeting women and having contact and fun. Recruiting is like a savings account. It's a long-term investment but it's the most rewarding and provides the greatest amount of income over the long term. It's not only our future or our retirement; it's also the American Dream.

How many parties should you hold each week?

3–4 each week.

What about bookings? How do you get bookings?

Show the benefits to the client. Make the hostess your business partner and reward her for each booking that is the result of her party. Keep in mind: One booking maintains, two bookings ensure, but three or more bookings grow and explode the business.

How about your hostess? How do you coach her?

This is one of my strengths because I believe this is essential for success. The hostess gives me names and addresses of who she is going to invite. I send and pay postage on reminder cards and give the hostess incentives (discounts on products) to follow up with invitees with a phone call. I ask the hostess to identify three guests that I choose randomly from her list with a "star" on their postcard. I also do "kitchen coaching" once I arrive at her home. This is reviewing with her what her rewards can be based upon her party's results, talk to her about becoming a consultant, etc.

How do you get most of your sales? (Internet, parties, one-on-one, etc.)

Over 75% of my sales come from holding parties and the other 25% come from re-orders.

How do you develop leads for your business?

This is not my strength. I don't do trade shows, cold calls, etc. Approximately 99% of my business comes from bookings that create bookings. I find the other avenues are more time-consuming and require so much more follow through.

What is your primary marketing method?

Holding what we call "Pampering Parties." Jafra as a company doesn't do advertising. They have built their company all over the U.S. and in 20 countries primarily by referral. I do excellent client service follow through and periodic mailings and email product specials to clients.

What advice can you give on joining local leads and business groups?

I've been there and done that and generally find that it is very time-consuming and doesn't produce the results fast enough. It is a good avenue if a consultant wants to expand her horizons in other areas.

What tips can you give about advertising? Has it worked for you?

Generally no. It costs to do this and you don't know who will respond to the ad. I prefer referrals from satisfied clients.

Give some tips about inventory...does a new consultant need a lot?

No. I want them (consultants) making money right away and seeing success. Excess unnecessary inventory can cause stress and panic and many times makes them feel premature defeat. I also do a "Starter" or "Grand Opening" party for my new consultants. I give them all the bookings and split the profit with them so they can invest their portion of profit in any stock or supplies they need.

What is your advice for recruiting and building a strong team? How do you manage them?

By being a role model and having them see that I "walk my talk." I hold at least two training meetings each month, respond immediately to phone calls, send out informative emails with information and training several times a month, have an open invitation to my consultants to come with me to my Pampering Parties so that they can train and observe. Most importantly, I use the "ping pong" approach. I "ping" information and guidelines for success to them and when they "pong" it back to me with interest, desire, initiative and results, then the back-and-forth continues.

What are your most important learning experiences?

Focus on personal business first. Everything comes from this including sales, bookings, recruiting, training and developing. Similar to when you toss a stone into a pond—everything ripples out from there.

Tips about motivation…how have you kept yourself motivated in order to rise to your professional level of success?

I've learned to be self-motivated. I like short-term goals (whether they are Jafra incentives, such as prizes and trips, or are my personal goals) and long-term dreams with a due date. I generally just try to compete with myself and increase numbers or growth each month over the same month the previous year.

What are your top tips for a fun, profitable party?

Put the focus on the hostess and the guests there. It is more important to know their names and to make them feel good, than it is to know every detail about the products that are being presented. Have fun, be brief and be gone…and if so, they will come back for more!

What advice can you offer to someone looking for a direct sales company to join?

Find a company that has products that you enjoy and can feel comfortable sharing. The best business is a "consumable" product business because you make instant profit and people will re-order in the future. Research to make sure that the company has a good hostess program which will create bookings and that the management program is achievable and lucrative for their future.

What about strategies for success? In your opinion, what will help someone succeed in a direct sales business? Many start, but only a few will attain success while others drop out. Why?

Answered in various questions above, but they need to be able to learn self-discipline and to take the work steps involved in order to have their dream. Too many think it is going to be too easy and they don't invest in themselves with training and doing the "daily disciplines" such as making a contact list, and making consistent phone calls to build their client base. At the first challenge or the first disappointment, they give up rather than reaching out to their Manager or Sponsor and asking what they can do differently in order to become successful.

What about managing your day-to-day business? How do you stay focused on growing your business when laundry needs to be done or other distractions beckon?

By having a "to do" list and trying your best to stick to the priorities that will build your business. There will always be distractions, but ask yourself "Does this really need to be done now?" or "Is this an effective use of my time?" *Is it building work or is it busy work?* If it is busy work, then try to delegate it—whether it is paying someone such as a high school student to help part-time or involving members of your family to help so that your business truly can be a family business where they cannot only contribute, but also feel a part of the success and feel good about the benefits received.

❧

Market everywhere! The more marketing sources you have, the more leads you will have coming in! Ask this simple question of show guests *"Have you ever thought of having a home-based business?"* Teach new team members to recruit right away. It instills confidence and keeps them excited! *Tracey P., Utah*

NOTES:

Interview:

Sue Whited

Company: Mary Kay Cosmetics
Title: Senior Sales Director
Where: Lakewood, CA

You don't have to look hard to understand why Sue is at the top of her game. She has provided interesting and thoughtful answers in her interview which point to why she is also a strong team leader. One only has to look at her endurance and passion for her business to understand why she is where she is.

How long have you been with your company?

Since 1987

How long have you been at your present level?

7 years

How large is your sales team?

45

Tell us about yourself

I am married with one daughter. I love to read, swim, walk, garden and study my Bible.

Briefly describe your company (objective, services, products, etc.)

Mary Kay Cosmetics is the number one brand of skin care and cosmetics for nine years in a row. Not only do we have the products to keep women looking young, but we have the best career opportunity. It can be life changing. We praise women to success.

What do you like best about your job?

I enjoy helping women develop their potential and build their self-esteem.

Have you worked with any other direct sales companies?

I have been with two other companies: A jewelry company for two years and another cosmetics company for two years. I enjoy Mary Kay's products and compensation plan more than either of those.

What principles have you followed to reach your current position with the company?

My top principles are persistence, consistency, keeping a positive attitude and following Mary Kay's principles of God first, family second and career third.

What mistakes have you made?

My mistakes have been procrastination, not thinking big enough and poor time management. I think if I could do it over, I would definitely set much bigger goals for myself and not give in to negativity.

What are your top sales tips?

Romance the products. Find the customer's need and fill it. Know your products very well. Book a facial and then have her invite several friends to share the makeover. Sell the sizzle! In my business it is essential to have an adequate inventory on-hand at all times to service my many customers. They deserve the best service and filling their orders immediately does that. Also, I totally believe that my products are the best in the marketplace and people can tell that I believe that.

What are your top recruiting tips? What helps you recruit?

Listen, listen, listen. When recruiting, go for quality, not quantity. Don't be selfish. We need to share what our company can do for them. I do a recruiting interview right after the makeover. Also, inviting guests to a Mary Kay party helps.

What have you earned at the company (trips, cars, prizes, etc.)

I have earned the use of five free cars. I have also earned five diamond rings from being in the National Court of Retail Sales (top level).

What words of advice can you give to a consultant who really wants to grow their business?

Give at least five business cards out every day. Get out and see the people and do skin care classes. Give excellent customer service. Also, have total belief in the company, the products and the opportunity you can offer. Always show enthusiasm for all of it.

What do you want to achieve next?

I would like to win the use of the Pink Cadillac. I would also like to be in the Court of Recruiting.

What do you enjoy most: Recruiting or sales? Why?

Sales! I enjoy helping a woman feel better about herself after we finish with the makeover. I love telling women about and sharing our products.

What about bookings? How do you get bookings?

I ask women for their opinion on our products. We call it "warm chatter"—meeting someone while you are out shopping and giving them your card. Also, guests from a skin care class who want to earn free products will book a party.

How about your hostess? How do you coach her?

This is very important. I give a hostess packet to the guest as soon as they book. Then I call her to keep her excited about what she's going to get free at her party.

How do you develop leads for your business?

I get referrals from existing customers. Sometimes I do a booth where I set up a display and get names.

What is your primary marketing method?

I do mailings. We have a program in Mary Kay that is called the Preferred Customer Program. Every three months my customers get a mailing with the latest brochure and it looks like it came directly from me. The next way is that I get out there where the people are and offer women a sample and my card. I always have materials ready to give out with me so no matter where I am I can offer my services to women. I always ask them if they already have a consultant and if they do I refer them back to her.

What advice can you give on joining local leads and business groups?

I personally do not like to use this method. I do better by just walking up to someone and offering them my card.

What tips can you give about advertising? Has it worked for you?

No. I don't think it's worth the expense.

Give some tips about inventory...does a new consultant need a lot?

It depends. I tend to encourage them to start around $1,800. I have found if they start with a huge inventory they will panic if they don't start selling it right away. I do feel they need inventory because people want their products right there at the show.

What is your advice for recruiting and building a strong team? How do you manage them?

My motto is: Attract not attack. People will be drawn to you when they see your enthusiasm and excitement. Share your opportunity with everyone and don't pre-judge! I listen to them and look for clues to find their need and then I share how being with Mary Kay can fill it.

You have to paint them into the picture and show them how they will benefit by being a consultant. Then once they are signed up, I work with them with training and we have weekly success meetings. I also do a monthly newsletter to keep in touch as well as sending them post cards and emails and phone them. I show them what to do but I don't do it for them. I always praise them for where they are and encourage them to go for bigger goals. In some cases, I believe in them before they believe in themselves!

What are your most important learning experiences?

You can achieve anything you want if you are willing to work for it and to never give up! Don't dwell on past failures; make it a learning experience for the future. Know that as long as you don't quit you are a winner! I have learned that people may not remember what you say, but they will remember how you make them feel. I have learned to always treat people the way I want to be treated. I think that is why I have such a loyal customer base.

I learned a long time ago not to blame anybody and to accept responsibility for where you are right now. It's the daily decisions we make that determine where we will be a year from now. I've also learned that no matter what happens we have the choice about how we deal with it.

Specifically, years ago I had a time in my life that I was so ill that I had to spend months in bed recovering and I used that time to really study and learn everything in my consultant's guide. I also learned how to sell without even leaving my sick bed by using the phone to call my customers. I had some of my very highest sales weeks. So I learned that it is your attitude more than the physical shape you are in that will determine your success!

Tips about motivation…how have you kept yourself motivated in order to rise to your professional level of success?

I listen to Mary Kay tapes or DVDs everyday. I read positive books. I watch my attitude and I don't hang around negative people. Set a goal and have an action plan. Know your purpose to keep you on-track.

What are your top tips for a fun, profitable party?

I have fun. I am very relaxed and I go with the attitude that whether they buy or not, I am going to have good time. People can tell when you are uptight so I leave any problems at home and I am a ray of sunshine! People have their own problems; they don't want to hear about yours. I also use humor in my presentation and the guests laugh and have a good time.

I really know my products and they want them because they have learned about the benefits of using them. Have complete sets ready to give each guest. You have to assume the sale. Don't be afraid to ask for the sale at the end; they are expecting you to ask.

What advice can you offer to someone looking for a direct sales company to join?

I personally believe that it's best to go with a company that has products that are consumable because my re-order business is a major source of my income. Also, make sure your commission is at least 50% as mine is.

What about strategies for success? In your opinion, what will help someone succeed in a direct sales business? Many start, but only a few will attain success while others drop out. Why?

I think the major cause of people dropping out is that they don't take the time to learn about their products and go to the trainings available. You have to commit to learn and not even think about quitting for at least a year from signing up. I tell people right when they sign up: *This is work.* Your success doesn't happen by magic and you will get out of it what you put into it. The most successful people I know have an inner drive that no matter what happens they will keep on going.

What about managing your day-to-day business? How do you stay focused on growing your business when laundry needs to be done or other distractions beckon?

I personally work with people from 8:30 a.m. to 8:30 p.m. The other hours are for household chores and errands and such. I have a *Six Most Important* list that I work from every day and I also have a weekly plan sheet because I do have a problem with the time getting away from me. I always ask my new clients if I can call them at work and that helps to free up my time at night. I make very quick and to-the-point calls so they don't mind me calling them at work.

Any final tips or ideas?

I believe that attitude is 90% and skills are 10%. Have a bounce-back ability no matter what happens. Get over it and move on. I don't let other people push my buttons. I am in control. I have learned that when you control your emotions you can control your paycheck!

In recruiting, I find what works best is to be persistent, don't give up, have fun doing it. Also, by being myself and being truthful. *Louise C., North Carolina*

NOTES:

Your Dream Day:
A Mini-Plan for Success

Excerpt from the Direct Seller's Boot Camp

When researching ideas to help you build your business, you are often counseled to write a business plan. You may think to yourself "Yeah, I really should write one. I'll do it one day." Then you skip by it and look for something easier, quicker; something you can do now. Perhaps there is something just as important that doesn't take as much research and effort as writing a business plan. While nothing will take the place of a well-thought out and formal business plan, there is something you can do now which has a similar effect. It's a very simple, very easy task that can get you started in a plan that helps you start building your business. It's called writing your "Dream Day" and it's a simple, yet deceptively powerful technique.

When doing this task, be sure to have some quiet time to yourself. This is a time for you to really decide what it is you want. You should take this time to be alone, free from disturbances. The reason for this task is to secure a mental image for yourself that you will be able to refer to again and again. This image will be a picture of your life exactly as you wish it to be. Although it isn't a traditional business plan, it has the power to become the one plan that keeps you moving forward since it is so easily referred to at any time.

Your dream day business plan incorporates a technique that will be as if someone took a snapshot of you living your dream life. It will only be of a moment in time, but after completing this task, you will understand that it will be of a moment that you feel your life is just as you want it to be. It will include you, your family, friends, business, possessions, feelings, etc. Be honest and clear about your answers and write notes down in order to be able to complete the final task of writing a complete snapshot. This is a simple task but you must do it completely for it to help you.

Defining Your Dream Day

To complete this assignment, you should be completely mentally free. Be by yourself without any other distractions (phone, TV, kids, etc.). Now, just imagine a day in your perfect life. How do you look? Be very descriptive: What are you wearing? What is your hair, body, clothing like, etc.? Where are you? What are you doing? Who is with you? How are you feeling? How are your companions feeling? Are you active or relaxing? Are you eating, drinking, laughing, etc? What is your home like? What about your car? Do you travel often? Do you want to? Do you have many friends or just a few close ones? Do you have many material items or are these unimportant? What is the weather like? Are you inside or outside? Are you shopping, swimming, working, etc? Where are you living? What does your dream life look like?

Write down a description of what your life is like at that moment in time when you feel you have accomplished success. It may just be a moment with your family relaxing out by your pool or a snapshot of you with friends skiing in an exotic location. Picture what it is and everything else about your life as you wish it to be at that moment.

Remember, this is a day in your *dream* life. You can be realistic or as far-reaching as you wish. Picture yourself captured in a split-second photograph that you would be able to look upon and feel that your dreams had been achieved. It doesn't mean you had no dreams after the picture was taken; only that at the time of the photo, your dreams up to that moment had been largely achieved. It should be a moment of happiness and contentment—whatever that is for you.

Next, work on your dream day business plan. What is your dream day in your business? How does it run every day? What tasks do you do? Describe a dream day running your business. Be as honest as possible. If you could paint a picture of you in your perfect day of running your business, what would it look like? Be very clear. For example it may look like this:

> "I'd get up at 7:00 a.m. and have freshly brewed coffee and fresh fruit. I get the kids off to school. Then I check my email and go over my daily activity calendar and return a couple of phone calls. At 8:30 a.m. I would jog or do yoga, then shower. My maid would be clearing the

breakfast dishes and starting on the laundry. (This is a DREAM DAY, after all.)

At 10:00 a.m. I am showered, dressed and at my desk, preparing a mailing. I take three phone re-orders totaling $150.00, counsel a client on new products we offer, and write a few emails to let clients know their products are shipping today. At 12:30, I have lunch on the patio. The sun is shining and it's a beautiful day. I have a lobster salad and iced tea. I read the daily paper and relax for a few minutes. I finish and freshen up for my afternoon meeting with a potential new recruit. We meet for coffee and she signs up. We plan to meet the following day to start her training.

I return home in my new silver convertible Jaguar the company pays for. My children are home from school and I spend some time with them, talking about their day, laughing and planning an upcoming vacation. By 3:00 p.m. my part-time assistant has arrived and she and I work in the office packaging orders, checking email, working on my newsletter, and a mailing. I finish at 5:30 and spend some time with my children and husband and we eat at an early dinner. My assistant continues working until 6:00 p.m. preparing my case for my evening sales party.

At 6:00 I change and check my case for my 7:00 p.m. sales party. I have six guests plus a hostess attending so I make sure I put together a few good product packages. My assistant has assembled some recruiting packages for guests and special gifts for the hostess. I pack them in my case.

At 9:00, I return home with $500.00 in sales, one recruit, two new possible recruits, and another two bookings. I change into some new cashmere pajamas I bought with a bonus check, check in with the kids and say goodnight. I pour myself a cup of tea and watch TV with my husband. We chat about our day and spend some time together. I relax knowing I've had a productive and profitable day.

And so on…This plan can be tweaked to fit *your* particular dream and your schedule. Spend several moments thinking of what this would be. Then begin writing a complete picture scenario of the moment. Be as descriptive as possible. Become very familiar with this photo. It will be valuable in helping you to instantly return to what it is that you want in life. When stresses and disappointments stack up against you, as they inevitably will, you can instantly recall this picture and remind yourself what you are working toward and what you need to do to make your life what you want it to be.

If you write it down it will help secure the mental snapshot you can refer to when you need a little motivation. When you know what you are working toward, it helps you keep moving. For some, it helps to hang pictures of things you want to purchase (a new car, a new house, etc.). If you have something solid in mind, you can focus on the tasks to get it easier.

Make this plan for your dream day business! Believe this: *If you can imagine it, you can build it.* It's very important to take the time to do this task. You will need it down the road. Get 20 minutes to yourself and start writing. DREAM BIG! Do it now and have some fun!

●

Interview:

Lisa Wilber

Company: Avon Products, Inc.
Title: Senior Executive Unit Leader
Where: Weare, NH

A true direct sales professional, Lisa isn't content to just sell and recruit. She has a priority of making a difference in people's lives. She does it with her seminars and her Avon business. Those who know her say Lisa is, in many ways, old school meaning this as a high compliment. She still puts her people and their goals first. Her understanding of success is easily translated to anyone who listens to her story. She has accomplished everything that direct selling/network marketing promises. And, just like many successful business builders, she's not done yet.

How long have you been with your company?

I started with Avon in 1981

How long have you been at your present level?

Since March 1994

How large is your sales team?

2,000+

Tell us about yourself

I've been married to my husband, Doug Wilber, since 1987. We have no children unless you count our four cats: Larry, Stinky, Lucky and Rocky. We lived for 15 years in a trailer park in Weare, New Hampshire and thanks to Avon we were able to move last year into a house that Doug built himself, with *no mortgage*. (Doug drew the plans for the house and even cut down the trees and milled the logs himself.) My hobbies are reading, writing and travel.

Briefly describe your company (objective, services, products, etc.)

Avon Products, Inc. has been in business since 1886 and is a Fortune 500 direct selling company with an army of Avon Representatives worldwide that total over 4 million with annual sales of $6.8 billion. In addition to makeup and skin care, Avon also sells jewelry, gifts, bath lines, intimate apparel, toys, vitamins and many other consumable products. Avon has offered a multi-level compensation plan since 1990 in the United States and is now expanding the option worldwide.

What do you like best about your job?

I like working with motivated people and helping them make changes in their lives and watching them succeed in achieving their goals. In particular, I like working with Avon because of the history of the company. Women could sell Avon and earn money before they could vote. Also, the very first Avon Representative, Mrs. P.F.E. Albee, is from my state of New Hampshire.

Have you worked with any other direct sales companies?

I've sold and recruited for Avon Products, Inc. since I was 18 years old. I worked for them part-time between 1981–1986, and then in 1987 I started full-time. When I was part-time, I also sold for other various other companies. I stopped all affiliations except with Avon when I went full-time because of something I heard at rally from a top earner with one of the other companies I worked with at the time. He said "you can't chase more than one rabbit" and I thought that sounded like that made a lot of sense. I decided to focus all my attention on one company and Avon was the one that I chose.

What principles have you followed to reach your current position with the company?

1. I refused to quit.
2. Focused like a laser on my goals and dreams.
3. Put my downline members' interests' as my top priority.

4. Treated this like a business.

5. Understood that my personal growth would determine my income.

What mistakes have you made?

I think my biggest mistake was not realizing that you can't drag people down the road of success. They have to want it—you can't want it for them more than they do. You have to be willing to say "NEXT" and move on to someone else who is willing to work.

In your opinion, what does it really take to achieve your level of success?

Above all else, it takes persistence. That plus an unwillingness to give up, no matter what the obstacle.

What are your top sales tips?

1. Make sure that everyone within 10 miles of you knows what you do.

2. Watch what other reps from other companies do in your area to promote themselves and try and find ways to incorporate that into your direct sales business. (For example, lettering your vehicle).

3. Be a walking advertisement by wearing the company name/logo on hats and shirts and by wearing a name badge or promotional button all the time.

What are your top recruiting tips? What helps you recruit?

1. Ask yourself: If I were looking for a job in my area, where would I look? Then *be* in those places. (Example: Run a classified line ad in the help wanted section of the newspaper).

2. Have a goal of how much recruiting information you will give out in a day and then stick to it day in and day out. (For example: Place three posters on bulletin boards per day; give three recruiting videos to three different people I meet during the day.)

3. Change your thinking from "looking for customers" to "looking for customers or recruits." Make sure that you offer every person both options.

I also find recruits by classified line ads in newspapers under the Help Wanted section. I also get many recruits from posters on bulletin boards and other marketing that I do.

What have you earned at the company (trips, cars, prizes, etc.)

I've earned 18 trips: Two for personal sales, one for an award-winning marketing idea and 15 for my multi-level marketing team success. I'm currently the number two money earner nationwide with Avon Products. I've earned the car allowance bonus from Avon since March, 1994. I have eight bookcases of local, regional and national awards too numerous to list. In 2004 my downline team sold over $10 million. Outside of Avon, I was nominated for the 2004 Athena Foundation Award and was named the 2004 Direct Selling Women's Alliance Ambassador of the Year. I've been a professional member of the National Speakers Association since 1998 and a supplier member of the Direct Selling Association since 2003 with my own company The Winner In You. (www.winnerinyou.com)

What words of advice can you give to a consultant who really wants to grow their business?

Be prepared to stick it out for the long haul. Avoid negative people and dream killers. Figure out *exactly* what you want and how bad you want it. Don't be wishy-washy about your dreams and goals. Work harder on your personal growth and development than you do on any other thing you do. Read, read, read.

What do you want to achieve next?

I have a goal to earn $1 million in one year. I also want to max out Avon's car allowance which requires six executives or above in my first generation. I currently have five.

What do you enjoy most: Recruiting or sales? Why?

I enjoy both, but recruiting is more rewarding emotionally in the long term. In my Avon downline, I have six senior executives plus myself for a total of seven on my team. There are only 75 in the entire company—so 10% are from my team. It's just a great feeling knowing that so many people have been able to achieve their goals and dreams through Avon and that I was able to help with that.

Which sales methods work best for you?

I look at my business like it is a matter of marketing. If I can get enough people to know what I do, I will sell products and recruit new representatives. So I do as many activities as possible to get as many people as possible to know what I do. Those are the marketing skills that I also teach to my downline members. (For example: place posters on bulletin boards, listing in the telephone book, classified line ads, wearing promotional buttons, lettering your vehicle, having an Adopt-a-Highway mile/sign.)

How do you develop leads for your business?

I use the marketing techniques, as I described above. We do collect contact information from as many people that we meet as possible so that we can follow up with a brochure mailing or send them a customer newsletter or information about joining our company.

What is your primary marketing method? (Mailings, referrals, cold calling, etc.)

Marketing has been the cornerstone of my group. Every activity is based on how many people we can let know what we do. The key, in my opinion, is relentless consistency. For finding potential recruits, our primary source of new recruits is classified line ads. For customers, it is a combination of many marketing activities including posters on bulletin boards, joining networking organizations, having a listing in the telephone directory, wearing a promotional button all the time, and more.

What advice can you give on joining local leads and business groups?

Don't bother joining local networking groups, Chamber of Commerce or professional business groups unless you are willing to show up at functions and participate in group activities. People will only start flowing your way after you have been around for a while and made your name synonymous with your company's name.

What about hostess coaching? What do you suggest?

I do not conduct parties as part of my business.

Give some tips about inventory…does a new consultant need a lot?

I do not believe that a new consultant should purchase a lot of inventory.

Tips about recruiting…what have you found that works best?

I run classified line ads in newspapers under Help Wanted.

Tips about motivation…how have you kept yourself motivated in order to rise to your professional level of success?

I read, read, read. I also constantly listen to audio programs about motivation, selling, management, marketing, and self improvement. I attend seminars and courses about my profession and industry. I attend classes given by my company but I also seek out learning opportunities outside the company. My favorite audio program: "Lead the Field" by Earl Nightingale. My favorite books: "See You at the Top" by Zig Ziglar and "The Miracle of Motivation" by George Shinn.

How do you get most of your sales? (Internet, parties, one-on-one, etc.)

I get most of my personal sales one-on-one, especially selling to people that I meet at businesses. I prefer to canvas businesses rather than houses because the people at businesses have income and you can see more of them at a time. I also like to use marketing to attract customers to me.

What is your advice for recruiting and building a strong team? How do you manage them?

When looking for recruits, look at the situation backwards: If you were looking for work today, where would you look? Then be sure to cover all places you come up with such as bulletin boards, classified line ads, job fairs, etc. Also come up with minimum qualifications that you require from your new downline members (whether or not they are required from your company) such as driver's license, checking account, telephone in their own name.

I require those things because I believe it is very hard to be a business owner and succeed without those minimum requirements. I prefer the word "partner" rather than "manager" when describing my relationship with my downline members. My job is to assist them in fulfilling their goals and dreams. I accomplish this by lots of communication including postal mail, email, telephone, and meetings. Recognition of achievements is high on my priority list. I recognize behavior I want to see.

What are your most important learning experiences?

Failures. When things go wrong or I don't get the results I wanted, I learn more.

What advice can you offer to someone looking for a direct sales company to join?

I personally prefer a company with a wide product line that doesn't focus on one or two trendy items. To me, "ground floor opportunity" means that a company hasn't proven its value yet in the marketplace. I also prefer companies with well known names and a solid history of positive name recognition.

What about strategies for success? In your opinion, what will help someone succeed in a direct sales business? Many start, but only a few will attain success while others drop out. Why?

Realize right from the start that this will be the hardest thing you've ever done. Work harder on your personal development than you do on earning a living and your income will soar. Read, read, read!

What about managing your day-to-day business? How do you stay focused on growing your business when laundry needs to be done or other distractions beckon?

I have a list of priorities that I work on every day. I say to myself "What are the most profitable things that I can do for my business today?" Without exception, working with people tops the list. Sometimes that includes customers, finding new customers or signing up a new recruit, and working with established representatives. My desk is generally a disaster area, but cleaning up my desk does not generate profits for my business.

What are your thoughts about a career in direct sales?

Nothing beats the freedom or the challenge of working in direct sales. You'll be harder on yourself than any boss you've had. Nothing beats the potential rewards: flexibility, unlimited income, travel incentives, recognition; no 9-to-5 job can match it. Being in direct sales has taken me from living in a trailer park, driving a Yugo and eating macaroni to being a millionaire!

In your opinion what do you think about the future of direct sales?

I believe direct sales will continue to grow and expand because of the relationship component of the business. Customers might shop the big box retailers for the price on some items, but when they want service and to trust who they purchase from, they turn to the direct sellers with whom they have built relationships.

Any final tips or ideas?

My website, www.winnerinyou.com, has a lot of free information that direct sales consultants can access. I have customer newsletters, downline newsletters, a screening script for prospects, and much more.

Five Points for Success

There are several marketing principles that many direct sellers neglect to apply to their business. **These are five basic, proven tips to develop your business.** They are as follows:

1. Stay Focused

If your focus is to sell products to make money, and essentially be a top seller, don't get side-tracked. Develop your leads, keep a good inventory (if your company works that way) and develop strategies to sell, get referrals, and keep your customers. If you are focused on recruiting, then don't worry about keeping every product in stock or developing events for sales. Your goals will be slightly different, but you will still need to get new leads. Determine what you want and stay focused on the *end* goal.

2. Niche Market Targeting

Who is your target customer? Who will most likely use your products/services? Can everyone use what you offer? Perhaps, but that doesn't mean everybody will want to consider it. By targeting a niche market you will separate the proverbial cream from the milk. You will immediately identify and market to those who will be your buyers and recruits more quickly and with less effort. Write a description of your ideal customer. Now, where will you most often find this type of person? This will tell you who you will focus your marketing efforts upon and where you may find your ideal customer.

What is a niche market? It is a group of potential customers who share common characteristics making them especially receptive to what you offer. For instance, perhaps you sell educational toys. Part of your niche market is parents—and breaking that down even further, probably mothers. You would target local moms and especially stay-at-home moms. Moms who do not work outside the house are proven to be very receptive to direct sales as a home-based work option.

If you sell health/nutritional products you could find a list of health club members who also subscribe to a magazine about starting a business. The combination of these two special interests will create a good niche market. By targeting your niche, you will get stronger leads that will be easier to turn into sales and recruits.

3. Produce Low Cost, Quality Leads

Prospects in your niche market are likely to be more interested in what you offer. Therefore, you'll be able to sign-up a higher than average percentage of the inquiries from them. Developing leads also allows you to collect contact information you can use to follow up with prospects who don't take action the first time they see your offer. For example, you can have potential customers and recruits go to your website where you may also offer a newsletter or free samples plus more information about the advantages of working with your company.

Once you have the prospect's email address you can follow up. Be consistent. An old adage of advertising is that prospects need to see a message 20 times or more before taking action. That requires consistency!

4. Create a Blazing Need

Emotion is proven to elicit more leads and recruits than logic. Your offers and other sales tools should play up the emotional rewards your prospect gets from using your company's products or by becoming a recruit. For example, to promote the business opportunity, describe how a successful recruit lives, how much they make, what their life is like, etc. Create a blazing need to begin enjoying this lifestyle.

Or perhaps you will focus on the sales of products. Let prospective recruits know how much items retail for as well as at the recruit discount. Seeing what they could save on their own products is often a very attractive way to recruit.

Another way to creative a blazing need is to offer a stellar promotion. Offering 10% off an item is OK, but a free gift with purchase and buy one, get one free offers will yield more sales. Remember, **keeping customers is a lot easier than finding new ones.** Give them something great to get them as a customer. Keep them by providing excellent service.

5. Inspire Action

Potential recruits and customers are people and people procrastinate. They get distracted by life and its responsibilities. Interest can start to fade and it may never happen. Encourage them by rewarding immediate action. One such idea is to offer a sign up bonus to new recruits—but *only* if they sign up within 48 hours of receiving your special offer. Perhaps you could offer a wonderful additional product package, marketing and training manuals or tapes and/or "start your own business kit" to new recruits if they sign up *now*.

Interview:

Christine Strong

Company: Taste of Home Entertaining, Launch Team as of 1/06
Title: Senior Director with Celebrations by Lillian Vernon (at time of interview)
Where: Rochester, NY

Christine's bubbly and happy personality came through in all of her communications with us. It's easy to tell she is a go-getter who works hard at developing her great business and growing team. She seems to maintain an "attitude of gratitude" that is an extremely admirable quality—and one that obviously serves her well in her business and in life.

How long have you been with Celebrations by Lillian Vernon?
Since October 2004

How long have you been at your present level?
Since April 1, 2005

How large is your sales team?
I have 440 in my downline.

Tell us about yourself

I'm a former Who's Who in residential real estate in North America, former EMT and Red Cross Instructor with over 1, 000 volunteer hours on an ambulance squad. I love Barbie dolls and play billiards with my husband. I'm also a proud mom of a seven year old boy.

Briefly describe your company (objective, services, products, etc.)

Life is a celebration. That's why we created Celebrations by Lillian Vernon™— to recognize and rejoice in the moments we experience every day…from the simple to the spectacular! We carry fresh, unique and hard-to-find items that will please all age ranges and celebrations. We offer free personalization and a 100% guarantee.

What do you like best about your job?

I like investing in people. The home party plan opportunity is the vehicle; I am the gasoline!

Have you worked with any other direct sales companies?

I was with another company in the early 1990s.

What principles have you followed to reach your current position with the company?

1. Show potential customers, hosts and recruits "what's in it for them." Find the prospect's WIIFM (what's in it for me?) principle.

2. Do your homework. Read direct selling books from the library, visit the leaders in the field via websites, continually learn and improve yourself.

3. Promote your business using car magnets, fliers, business cards, label pins, signature in emails telling about your business/story. Also, a helpful site is www.thebooster.com, etc.

What mistakes have you made?

I made the mistake of not ordering enough materials for prospecting when I began. I realized you have to invest to profit. I learned business is where you find it; it doesn't come to you.

In your opinion, what does it really take to achieve your level of success?

Have a plan to execute. Most people have a goal but don't have the steps outlined to achieve the goal.

What are your top sales tips?

Always "upsell." When someone gives you their order, review it and find a compatible item to offer that will complement their purchase. For example, if someone orders a paper towel rack, be sure to offer them the napkin holder to go along with it.

What are your top recruiting tips?

Wear your nametag at all times. Don't be afraid to talk to your friends about the opportunity. Run internet (Google.com) ads. *Most* important: Create a system that is can be easily duplicated and teach it to your downline to keep the chain going.

Also, you can give your prospect a *Top Ten Reasons to Join* list. Present your home party plan information in an impressive binder. Be sure to include a biography listing on yourself about why you joined and why it was the best decision for you. Most people want to join under a successful person and one whom they will have confidence in for training and guiding them. Make your binder a scrapbook of sorts with photos of parties, kit displays, the best promotions the company has run in the past, any achievements you have reached within the company, etc.

What have you earned at the company (trips, cars, prizes, etc.)

I am the number three recruiter in the company and currently I am earning a trip to Disney World. I also received smaller items such as leather baggage set, business and office supplies, etc.

What words of advice can you give to a consultant who really wants to grow their business?

Get training from the experts in the field. Do a web search of home party plan trainers and attend seminars; get training materials from those who have succeeded and will show you the steps to follow.

What do you want to achieve next?

I'd like to have a consultant in every state (46 states currently), a multi-million dollar producing team with this year ($900,000 and counting!).

What do you enjoy most: Recruiting or sales? Why?

I really enjoy recruiting. The leadership role is one that I value. It is rewarding for me to see others achieve success when I was a part of it (helping them get there).

How many parties should you hold each week?

I recommend at least three each week.

What about bookings? How do you get bookings?

Offer free gifts and discounted products in a fun environment instead of asking them to do you a favor to hold a party for you—it's all in your approach and confidence.

How about your hostess? How do you coach her?

Be sure to call her, give guidance and follow up the day before the party and the day of the party. Have good communication with her. Be sure to ask her if she ever considered doing what you do and follow up after the party and ask if she thought it was fun and easy. Then ask her if she could use $$$ per week. Tell her if she joins tonight, this could be considered her grand opening party!

How do you get most of your sales? (Internet, parties, one-on-one, etc.)

Parties

How do you develop leads for your business?

Advertise locally for hosts. I've also developed leads by offering free and discounted gifts to those who host a Celebrations by Lillian Vernon Party. Advertise nationally (web) for consultants. Also by offering training and support through a private team website with chat room, file sharing, and calendar of events.

What is your primary marketing method?

I run advertising on work-at-home mom websites.

What advice can you give on joining local leads and business groups?

Be friendly and approachable when you join a group. Be sure to have business cards available at all times when you attend functions and keep your "pitch" to two minutes or less. Know that if you expect people to network with you, you should also network with them first.

What tips can you give about advertising? Has it worked for you?

Be sure you don't spend all your money in one place. For example, I have had more leads by spending my monthly ad budget placing ads in six different smaller-sized work-at-home mom sites than I did when spending the entire budget on one big ad on one site.

Give some tips about inventory…does a new consultant need a lot?

Our company doesn't require you to stock inventory.

What is your advice for recruiting and building a strong team? How do you manage them?

Give your team attainable sales goals in the beginning to keep up their morale. Always find something to reward everyone on. Talk to them about how you want them to be. Let them know you think they are smart, enthusiastic, focused…they will want to please you and keep up that reputation.

What are your most important learning experiences?

Your family comes first, then your business. Make time for your loved ones, because money comes and goes, but they will be around to love you, rich or poor. Working at home can easily overtake so much from your family time, so in my experience, setting yourself a work day schedule (and off time) is vital to your overall performance and happiness.

Tips about motivation…how have you kept yourself motivated in order to rise to your professional level of success?

I look for internet sites like to help my business grow. I like:

www.stepintosuccess.com
www.karenphelps.com
www.isellmoretoday.com
www.thebooster.com
www.lemonaidlady.com

What are your top tips for a fun, profitable party?

Wear funky, fun clothes when you go—something bright and lively with crazy patterns (think along the lines of a clown). Because when you have their attention and they know you are there to have fun, the atmosphere is light-hearted from the beginning.

Make the hostess feel like a princess. Get a crown and scepter from your local party store. Make the hostess wear the crown the entire night and praise her and give her gifts throughout the night. Her friends will tease her about the crown, and be envious of all the attention and freebies she is receiving that night.

What advice can you offer to someone looking for a direct sales company to join?

Interview your sponsor. Don't just join under someone who has an ad out there. Know how invested that person will be in helping you become a success.

What about strategies for success? In your opinion, what will help someone succeed in a direct sales business? Many start, but only a few will attain success while others drop out. Why?

My best strategy for success is to get trained! Like a doctor would for his industry, you too should get as much training as possible. The first place I like to start with my team members is to have them find the book by Joyce M. Ross, *DIRECT SALES: Be better than good, be great.* It has lots of basic tips for the industry and for a beginning consultant.

What about managing your day-to-day business? How do you stay focused on growing your business when laundry needs to be done or other distractions beckon?

Set a schedule including what days you will take off. Then let everyone you sponsor (and your family) know what your "work hours" are. Be sure that some of those hours are in the evening a few days a week, so that when you do have leads who work during the day, you can still connect with them without interfering with dinner or kids' bed times. I like to schedule my family appointments in the calendar for the month in one color and then fill in any parties and work hours in another color.

Any final tips or ideas?

A successful man is one who can lay a firm foundation with the bricks others have thrown at him.—David Brinkley

Family and friends can be your best support or your worst critics. Be sure you know what you want to do and what you believe in, so no matter what feedback you get, you know in your heart you are doing what is right for you!

☙

Have goal-setting and determination to make it no matter what the cost. Really work your business everyday and find out what things you can do to have the greatest impact on your business that day. While doing that, teach others to do the same and realize they have goals and dreams like you. This business could be just what they need and I will help them every step of the way. *Wendy H., Arizona*

NOTES:

Marketing Tips

Excerpt from PUMP News Guides

Slow Movers?

Do you keep inventory? If you do, you probably have a bin (or two) of slow-selling products. Maybe they were promotional, seasonal or limited-time products you stocked up on, but that didn't sell as you had hoped.

Get them out of your inventory by giving them away free with the purchase of product packages. Or offer a grab bag of items for $1.00 each at your parties. Give some to new recruits to thank them for joining your team. If you do this at least three times a year, you should be able to keep your inventory down to just top selling items and get your slow sellers off your hands.

Buy Me, Buy My Products

When you sell your products, you are also selling you. You need to make that clear to your customers. When they make a purchase from you they are purchasing your expertise, your knowledge on the market of products you sell and your future service. Be sure to let them know that when they buy from you, they will receive complimentary product updates, notices on promotions, your free newsletter, a gift during their birthday month, whatever...

People like to buy from people they feel really appreciate the business. Make your customers know how much they are appreciated by staying in touch and keeping them in the loop on new items, etc. They will be more open to becoming a repeat customer whey they feel they are appreciated. Receiving a thank you note after the sale is a great way to start.

Think about it: How many thank you notes have you received recently from vendors you've done business with? How many actually followed up with a phone call asking how the product is working for you? We'll bet you remember them the next time you need some products. Be that vendor who gets remembered and referred.

Direct Sales Charity

Working with other direct sellers in your area to raise money for charities can be a wonderful way to get attention for your business as well as do something for others. By holding different quarterly events, you can get other sellers to donate their products and services for raffle drawings, get some good press for your businesses and do something charitable.

Donate a portion of the sales generated during the events. Be sure to let attendees know what portion will be donated. People are more likely to spend more freely when they know it is going to a good cause. Be sure to send out announcements to your local papers to help get some publicity.

You can post a copy of the cancelled check sent to the charity on a website for anyone interested to view after the event. This will let your participants and attendees know how much was generated and that the check was actually sent. After the event, send another announcement to local newspapers, etc. to let them know your event was a success and how much money you raised for the charity. *NOTE:* Be sure to black out/cover up any personal information on your check including your account number, etc. before posting it to your site.

&

Interview:

Michelle Pendergrass

Company: AtHome America
Title: Bronze Star Executive
Where: Knox, IN

Michelle is a solid source of inspiration. Her responses to our questions are thoughtful and well-intentioned. She not only maintains and grows her business at enviable levels, but she makes a point of doing it with honesty and integrity—something you can sometimes only find when dealing with a caring direct sales professional, like Michelle.

How long have you been with your company?

3+ years

How long have you been at your present level?

10+ months

How large is your sales team?

44 members

Tell us about yourself

I am a wife, a mother of a six-year old son, a homeschooler, a Women's Ministry leader, and a writer. These passions consume my life and I couldn't be happier!

Briefly describe your company (objective, services, products, etc.)

AtHome Amercia's mission statement coupled with the founding sister's passion to change lives sets this company apart. The focus is and has always been on God first, followed by family, and then AtHome America. The goal is to change America one heart, one home, one family at a time. We strive to enhance lives spiritually, personally, and professionally. We do so first by our own example, our career opportunity, our homewares, and our website. We have a strong commitment to family values. We believe that we are an important contributor in the greater opportunity to improve the quality of life in the United States of America.

All of these things listed are taken from the mission statement sisters Lisa Brandau and Becky Wright live out loud. They didn't just write down words, they are the examples of these words. AtHome America makes you know you are important. The homewares we sell seem such a distant second to the purpose. They are beautiful and of the utmost quality. But in life, what matters most is people and I've found by first-hand experience that the people at this company care about the people.

What do you like best about your job?

Direct sales affords opportunity that very few careers can claim: Control. My job grants me the ability to structure my family's day based solely on the needs of my family—during any season of our lives. I am not under the constraints of a typical career. I am free to put God at the forefront of my business. I am free to put my family next, and then I can "go to work." Instead of revolving my family around my job, I have the freedom to meet my family's needs before thinking about heading to the "office."

Have you worked with any other direct sales companies?

No.

What principles have you followed to reach your current position with the company?

My position is a result of three basic elements: Integrity, honesty, and determination. Integrity lends the idea of adhering to strict moral and ethical codes, of being complete, whole, and of being unimpaired. I want my guests to be confident and assured that they're getting no less than 100% from me. It is my goal to enhance the lives of those I have contact with. Honesty in all situations is the proving ground for integrity. Determination is the driving force of your purpose.

What mistakes have you made?

The biggest personal mistake I made was not setting a concrete purpose for my business. The purpose evolved over time and in retrospect, a lot of trials could have been avoided if I would have simply known why I was doing this job.

The biggest tactical mistake I made was my total lack of follow up. Once I learned how important it was to follow up and follow through, things started flowing with great ease.

In your opinion, what does it really take to achieve your level of success?

Determination is simply a firmness of purpose, a resolve. At the same time, it is defined as fixed movement or a tendency toward an end. The end that I move toward with my business is detrimental to success. There must be a goal. Whether it is a spiritual goal, a personal goal, or a monetary goal, there must be a clear motivation. I have not already reached my goal, but I make every effort to take hold of it. I run with endurance keeping my eye on the goal. The "fixed movement" of determination takes hold of the goal and claims it as victory while still running.

What are your top sales tips?

People today are busy. Everything is faster and more convenient. We must, at all times, respect the time of our clients. Keep things short, simple and practical. Think in terms of bullet points on an outline. Most of all, though, have fun. Since people are so busy and stressed with the demands of the daily grind, when they get together with their friends they don't want another stressor. Make them feel appreciated and loved. Laugh with them, and share some of your embarrassing moments. Make it a point to try to somehow improve their lives with what you have to offer.

What are your top recruiting tips? What helps you recruit?

Learning to become a mentor instead of a recruiter has been monumental in my career with AHA. Nothing can build a stronger bond than spending time with the person you're mentoring. With a solid foundation built on the rock, the organization will withstand the storms. This is a business of relationships. I feel that without investing quality time in these relationships, you're spinning your wheels.

What have you earned at the company (trips, cars, prizes, etc.)

A Disney cruise.

What words of advice can you give to a consultant who really wants to grow their business?

I can't stress enough the importance of honesty. Be honest, first, with yourself and the goals you set out to achieve. Be real and be yourself. God made each one of us with a purpose and He loves every single one of us. Don't try to change who you are to make this business work. The business is flexible and pliable. You can mold it to fit your life and your personality. You can use your gifts and talents to soar above status quo.

Other people who have built successful businesses are great inspiration and are spectacular role models. But we cannot strive to be who they are. We must come to understand our God-given gifts and then act accordingly. You've heard this before: A gift isn't a gift until it is given away! (And you can't give away someone else's gift…you can only give away yours.) You are so precious as a person and you have so much to offer to others. It is vitally important to realize that each one of us is in this business for our own reasons.

What do you want to achieve next?

I'd like to reach the level of Silver Star Executive.

What do you enjoy most: Recruiting or sales? Why?

I like mentoring. I enjoy developing the relationships.

How many parties should you hold each week?

You should hold one or two *consistently*.

What about bookings? How do you get bookings?

I ask everyone. I try to make it a practice to call those who didn't attend and offer my services as well as ask if they'd like be spoiled. I also ask every guest in attendance.

When someone says no, a leader in my company taught me to ask, "No, not now?" or, "No, not ever?" Sometimes the present isn't the best time for the person and I may need to just ask when a good time would be. Then, of course, follow up.

How about your hostess? How do you coach her?

This is one of the most important parts of the business. Always keep in touch with your hostess and be sure to let her know the next time you're going to call and what you want her to do until that next call. Keep her informed and stay in contact with her often before the party.

How do you get most of your sales? (Internet, parties, one-on-one, etc.)

Home shows are the lifeblood of my business. Anything else is icing on the cake.

How do you develop leads for your business?

The leads for my business are on the invitation lists.

What is your primary marketing method?

I make phone calls to warm leads—those I've already met or talked to before.

What advice can you give on joining local leads and business groups?

I have not tried these.

What tips can you give about advertising? Has it worked for you?

Don't waste your money. It hasn't worked for me. It has been far more profitable to build relationships with my clients.

Give some tips about inventory…does a new consultant need a lot?

I don't carry inventory.

What is your advice for recruiting and building a strong team? How do you manage them?

The most important thing I've learned from painful mistakes is that no one does this business for the same reasons I do and no one runs their business the same way I do. Instead of expecting people to do just as I do, I offer guidelines and make sure they understand that I give options, not ultimatums. I want each member of my team to be successful…and we all have our own definitions of success.

You may want one show a week; I may want one show a month. If we each meet our individual goals, we are both successful. As a team leader I want to make sure I commend you for meeting your goals even though they are not the same as mine.

I take the time to get to know the leaders on my team. I give them guidelines for building leaders on their teams. I give them space to run their own businesses and I give them room to make mistakes and room to learn and grow. I let them know I care.

I don't think I so much "manage" them as much as I "mentor" them. I don't want my team to conform to my standards, I want them to grow and stand on their own. I want to nurture them and watch them bloom.

What are your most important learning experiences?

Unfortunately, there are many who have given direct sales a bad rap. Nearly everyone you talk to can tell you about a bad experience with some company out there. To overcome those stereotypes about us, we must always strive with diligence to meet and anticipate the needs of our clients. We should seek to serve all while being honest about all situations. If you made a mistake, admit to it and remedy it. If you forgot to order something, be honest and fix it. Go above and beyond what is normal. Make good customer service a practice of habit and your clients will be loyal.

Tips about motivation…how have you kept yourself motivated in order to rise to your professional level of success?

Sometimes it's hard to stay motivated. I try to always focus on the end result, the BIG goal. I try not to stumble on the little pebbles in the road.

What are your top tips for a fun, profitable party?

This is your business. You can let it control you or you can be in control. Take it upon yourself to send the invitations. Make sure the hostess has totally filled a guest list. Call the guests yourself and remind them to come to the event. Focus on meeting the individual needs of the guests. Keep it short and simple.

What advice can you offer to someone looking for a direct sales company to join?

Have peace when you make your decision. Take your time and find the company that fits you. Love the product and investigate the company. Make sure the company listens to their consultants. Ask questions. Expect answers.

What about strategies for success? In your opinion, what will help someone succeed in a direct sales business? Many start, but only a few will attain success while others drop out. Why?

Again, I stress the determination and the end goal. If every pebble is a boulder in your business, it is not likely you'll travel far along that road. If you lose focus on the end goal, you tend to stray off the road and those detours are sometimes really rough-riding.

What about managing your day-to-day business? How do you stay focused on growing your business when laundry needs to be done or other distractions beckon?

This is truly an area that has required me to learn the definition of discipline. You must constantly be aware of distractions. For me, learning which distractions were controllable was key. Controllable distractions include things like the phone, TV, and computer. My family is never a distraction. They are part of my purpose, so I let go of the idea that we must be on some strict unattainable schedule. I have learned to become more flexible. I have learned to control my time rather than letting it control me.

Your business should not ever consume all of your time. Your family's resentment will grow strong if your main focus is the business. Family time should be sacred. And your family should be able to see you living that model and teaching your new team how to do the same. The phone shouldn't ever pull you away from the dinner table, or away from reading that book to your child. When you make the effort to put your family first, your family will naturally support you when you do your shows or when you need an hour to make phone calls. Even young children understand where priorities lie.

When we talk about growing a business in conjunction with growing a family, we need to remember that the tall and mighty oaks start as acorns and take many years to come into maturity. A business that is an acorn today will be that mighty oak given time and nurturing. It will not grow into its might quickly. Patience, determination, and knowing the end result makes it easier to focus on the tasks at hand.

☞

My biggest mistake? Not being committed to my business from the very start.
Pam W., Arkansas

<u>NOTES:</u>

Have Shyness, Will Succeed

Salespeople come in many types. There are the extroverted, bubbly, irrepressible sales people. They are easy to like and will be happy to extol the virtues of their company to anyone—friend or stranger—without much prodding. Does this sound familiar?

Or, perhaps you are more of an introvert and shy, new to sales, or new to running your own business. Going up to strangers or talking about your business to everyone you meet during the course of your day is just not your style. You cannot imagine doing it. Does this sound like you?

Whichever personality you have, you can succeed in sales. Whether you are outgoing or shy you probably love your products and services and feel confident about sharing them with others. But how do you get the word out without the excruciating task of confronting strangers and calling everyone you know to hold a party?

Naturally, if you are very shy you need to come out of your shell at some point to talk about your business (or no one will ever know about you!). However, there are ways to do it without the terror non-salespeople have when they start out. If you cannot imagine talking to strangers to help open the door for you, you will need to find alternative methods to developing leads.

Whether you use the principles given to you by your team leader or research new ones, you will find a proven system to developing leads will pay off in all aspects of your business. Leads can be cold (meaning you have never met them) or warm (you have met the lead or spoken on the phone). Warm leads are obviously easier to sell and recruit. They already know you and know your business. You essentially are just following up with them. Nearly every salesperson prefers warm leads. (To learn more about getting lots of warm leads, read our *Direct Sellers Guide: Get Booked Solid!*)

Working Ideas

Here are a few lead-generating ideas that have been proven to work. They are inexpensive and will help get leads quickly and consistently.

Newsletters

Have you considered writing a newsletter for your target market? It's not a new idea; however, it can be used very successfully by direct sellers to get new leads, customers, etc. Newsletters are not difficult to produce and they can be easily updated monthly or quarterly. If sent electronically a newsletter can be extremely cost-effective and can reach a wide market. It should include various promotions and ads for your own business.

If a newsletter is well-written and contains useful information, it will be read, kept, and possibly even passed on to a friend. Use topics that hold interest for the reader and that make them want to open it. For example, if you sell food items or food storage items one possible newsletter idea would be:

Is It Still Good?
Simple Storage Ideas to Extend Food Freshness

People interested in food, cooking, etc. would be interested in this information. Research the topic (the web will be a great resource) and add more information inside, plus your ads, promotions, etc. You can do this for nearly any product and service. Offer the ability to view archives on your website. You should find it a very helpful sales tool!

You can print out a newsletter and mail it or do an electronic format and post it to your site. In your newsletter, always add a sales or recruiting promotion for your business (i.e., Join my team by the 31st and receive a free product package!). Include an expiration date on all promotions to inspire action.

Local Review Guide

Develop a list of local restaurants, shops, service providers, etc. that you frequent. Write a short review on your experience with each one (elicit the help of friends and their experiences, too!).

Keep it light and humorous and include those with which you have had several good experiences, as well as anything new in town that you've tried. Lay it out in a simple but attractive format. Add promotions for your business, print, and voila! You have a local guide that your customers will get a kick out of reading!

It does not need to be professionally printed. Make copies on a color printer. You can print them on glossy paper, add a few photos and distribute them at the local retailers that you have reviewed as well as on your website, etc. Get creative!

Welcome Baskets

Provide a gift basket to local realtors for their new home buyers. Add little goodies from your product line (maybe your newsletter or review guide, too?), plus catalogs, your business card, etc.

Promotional Materials

A little more costly, but really fun idea is to have t-shirts, coffee cups, decals, etc. printed up. Every customer who orders gets one. Most will use it. It's repeat marketing that keeps you in their mind.

Ballot Boxes

Tried and true for getting leads: Place ballot boxes in local retailers (salons, boutiques, etc.). Add a flier on a stand (acrylic flier stands to insert fliers are available at your local office supply). Run promotions on the flier to win a free gift basket, service, product, etc. Have a clear picture of what the prospect will win. Gather leads weekly or monthly. If it's a good offer and if you can get at least two or three retailers to co-operate, you will have a great source of leads! *Note:* Working with small, privately-owned shops and boutiques is the easiest way to get started.

Getting Referrals

Get great referrals! Send an email to all of your customers requesting the name of a referral who would like your services. Offer them a nice gift or certificate. Create a blazing need: Put a time limit on it. Ask for a referral in the next 24 hours. If you make it longer, they may forget. If they reply, mail them a small gift or email them a gift certificate which they can print out and use later. Don't forget a thank you card!

Use the same technique for feedback. Ask for it in a limited time frame for an immediate reward. Use your positive feedback in all of your marketing efforts.

Website

If your company allows it (and many do), set up a simple website. It doesn't have to cost much or be complicated. There are many free and low-cost services available where you can put together a simple site easily and in literally under an hour. Run monthly promotions where you advertise specials, offer free samples, talk about new products, etc. You can even hold a drawing for a free item.

Send a link to the site to your customers every month. Make each month different and interesting. You could do your newsletter online and promote it in your initial email link. If your customers come to expect quality information and great deals from visiting your site, they will be excited to get your monthly links!

Business Card Marketing

Magnetic business cards have been used successfully for several years from sellers of real estate to children's toys. Three more ideas to make sure people glance twice when you hand them your card:

- Make it noticeable! Punch a hole in the corner of your card and tie a small piece of ribbon into a bow.

- Place your card in a tiny plastic bag with a sample from your product line. People love samples and making it standard to give your card with a sample will increase the likelihood of them keeping it.

- State your message in standard business card format (horizontal) and add a small message vertically on one end "Can also be used as a bookmark!" People will turn it to read what it says and may just keep it around.

- Package your card with a small candy bar or wrapped chocolate. Tie them together with ribbon. Would you throw this away?

- Develop a Tip Calculator. Non-math whizzes struggle with how much a 15, 18, or 20% tip would be on a $35.00 meal. Put a simple tip calculator together for common purchase amounts; print them on stickers to put on the back of your business cards. You can even laminate them. People will keep these and use them over and over again!

Bookings…Get 'em!

Be sure to work all your sales parties with your products, literature, samples, and one more important item: Your calendar! When booking future sales parties while working a party, be sure to have a monthly calendar with days you will hold parties highlighted. Tell prospects that they can hold a party on any dates that are highlighted that are still free. Be sure some of the dates are already highlighted, creating a sense of urgency for people to book dates that are still free.

Having some booked dates will help inspire action. If someone is thinking of holding a party, get out your calendar and let them know what dates are free. Show them three or four free open dates only, not a whole month of available days. If you narrow down the choices, it will be easier to get them to book a date.

You may even offer to send out the invitations. This way you can take control over the event and you will be able to count on those who have responded favorably. This takes the stress off the hostess and gives you the ability to gather the prospects' names, addresses, phone, etc. That way, even if they don't show up for the party, you will still have their information to add to your mailing list as a new lead!

Offer special incentives for those who "book a party now!" Give special discounts, free gifts, etc. for anyone who books a party while at a sales party. This helps guests get excited about holding a party and can often get you more than one or two bookings. Offer them a small gift right now plus an extra special gift the day of the party. This two-gift approach gets them to act now, plus encourages them to go forward with actually holding the party for you. *Idea*: Ask them which item under $10.00 they like and which item at or under $25.00. Give them the $10.00 item now for booking and the $25.00 item when they hold the party.

Interview:

Chuck and Sherry Caza

Company: Time to Celebrate/House of Lloyd
Title: Leaders
Where: Ontario, Canada

Chuck and Sherry Caza are seasoned professionals—well regarded in the world of direct sales. They have built their business, several times, on a basis of ethical behavior, hard work, dreams, and determination. They are warm and outgoing people intent on helping people whenever and wherever they can. Their candid interview is definitely one in which many helpful ideas for growth, management and perseverance are revealed.

How long have you been with your company?

We started with Time to Celebrate in 2004 and have been with House of Lloyd Canada since 1991, and Richmont Direct since 2002.

How long have you been at your present level?

One year with Time to Celebrate, 10 years with House of Lloyd Canada, and four years with Richmont Direct.

How large is your sales team?

2,400 with House of Lloyd until its closure and many of our team stayed with us with Richmont Direct and Time To Celebrate

Briefly describe your company (objective, services, products, etc.)

We are currently with two different and distinct companies: Time to Celebrate and Richmont Direct. Time To Celebrate, which is a property of Department 56 out of Eden Prairie, MN. Time to Celebrate offers many exclusive products to help people celebrate life with friends and family everyday. Their wonderful year-round product line is designed around different stories to help you create memories and start traditions throughout the year. Each catalogue features products to enhance current holidays and other special times of the year. The products are fabulous and the company programs are wonderful.

Richmont Direct offers four different product lines from cooking accessories to Christmas and jewelry pieces. Both companies offer different product to enhance your life and enable you to grow your business.

What do you like best about your job?

We would be selfish to say the best part of our job is the ability to stay home and raise our kids. That is an honest answer but we also get as much joy in helping other people start their business and watching them grow. Over the years we have seen many people join our team as shy consultants and slowly emerge as strong leaders earning a six-figure income. We have helped several people do this by believing in them and helping where we can.

Have you worked with any other direct sales companies?

We worked for a wonderful party plan company out of Kansas City for 10 years until the owner passed away and the company closed. It was devastating, but we also knew we had the skills and the team to grow again if we could just find another company close to the values and product our customers were used to. We asked most of our team to join us when a new party plan company out of Plano, Texas opened. Richmont Direct was a good replacement and we were proud to be one of the first consultants with them.

In late 2004 we had the opportunity to join another very reputable company out of Eden Prairie, Minnesota, and have enjoyed every minute once again. Our newest business offers the products our customers are looking for, offers one of the best commission structures, and honestly tries to support each of us as we grow our business.

What principles have you followed to reach your current position with the company?

When we joined our first party plan company, we were constantly told that we should concentrate 90% of our time holding parties and 10% of our time growing our business through recruiting. This was good in theory but if we wanted to "grow" our business, we had to offer the business opportunity to everyone.

We slowly started recruiting and encouraged our new team members to do the same. As our team grew and moved up to leaders, we moved to Directors and eventually Executive Directors. We are using the same principles today to grow with our new companies and it is working. We are also strong believers in setting the pace and leading by example. If we are not working our business and recruiting everyday, how can we expect our team to do the same?

Our last belief would be honesty. If you are honest with yourself and your customers, then your business will grow. If you say you are trying to grow your business, but spend more time watching TV, are you being honest with yourself?

What mistakes have you made?

We have all made mistakes, as none of us are perfect. If we are honest and do the best we can, that is all anyone can expect from themselves or people on their team. As Managers, Leaders or Directors, the decisions that are made everyday may not be the answers that people like to hear but they are honest and given for reasons others may not understand.

Looking back, if we had to pick one big mistake, it would be not quitting our jobs and growing our business before we did! It is also very important to research the company you are looking to join and make sure they offer product and programs to encourage your friends/family and guests to purchase. It is also important to make sure they have a program in place to help you grow at your pace.

In your opinion, what does it really take to achieve your level of success?

To achieve any level of success, there must be a reason to *want* that success. Find that reason and you will succeed. We started out just trying to earn a "couple of dollars" for dinner once in a while and then realized very quickly if we grew our business and offered the opportunity to others, we would make more commission. More commission allowed us to quit our jobs, do more with the kids and spend more time and money growing our business. It was our desire to be self-employed that drove us to success.

Everyone must find a reason *why* they want to start their own business before they join any company and work towards those goals. Whether it is putting your kids through school, saving for retirement, earning fabulous trips or just getting out once in a while, ask yourself, what do I really want out of this?"

Take your business slowly and don't expect immediate success overnight. Find that drive and desire and be very patient. If you are with the right company, eventually your business will start to grow.

What are your top sales tips?

- Be honest with your customers.

- Create relationships with your customers through calls, cards, and keeping in touch. Let them know how much you appreciate their business.

- Join a company that offers the kind of products you can get excited about. Excitement breeds excitement, and your friends and family will want to know what all the excitement is about.

- Time will equal success. The more time you dedicate to your business, the more success you will have. There were many nights when we locked ourselves in our office and worked on the phones. We were determined to work as long as possible until we had three parties booked or one new team member.

What are your top recruiting tips? What helps you recruit?

Be honest with people interested in joining your team. Let everyone know all the great parts of joining your team, but also let them know there are areas for improvement as well. Be honest and don't "sugarcoat" the truth. If you are honest both ways, people will respect your honesty. You must sell yourself before you can sell anything else.

Again, build relationships. People we talk with today may never join our business or they may join next year. You just never know. Get people excited about the prospect of growing their own business and help them create that WANT.

Reach out to as many people as you can, and then follow up. Always let people know you are there to help them. Nothing is worse than joining a company and never hearing from the people who sponsored you.

Believe in the company you are with, believe in the product and programs, and most of all, believe in yourself. Show your enthusiasm and people will want to know about you and your business. Talk about your business and don't be shy!

We have met way too many consultants who never talk about their business. You never know when a perfect stranger is looking for a great part-time job. Don't be afraid of rejection! Ninety-five percent of the people you ask to hold a party or look at a recruiting package will turn you down. That is just the nature of this business.

Once you learn and accept that most people may not be interested in your company, you can move on and focus on all the people who *are* interested in learning more. If you are positive, smiling and knowledgeable about your business and people decide not to have a party or join your team, you need to quickly realize that they just might not be interested at this time and it is nothing personal. In this female-dominated world of party plan companies, you cannot take rejection personally.

Most people just don't realize the potential in growing their own business. Stay strong, positive, and focused. Keep talking about your business and make five to ten calls every day. Keep doing this and you *will* be successful.

What have you earned at the company (trips, cars, prizes, etc?)

We joined our first party plan company in 1991 and worked hard booking parties and growing our business. By 2001, when the owner passed away and the company closed, we had over 2,400 people in our lineage earning well over $500,000 per year. We were very fortunate to earn trips to Hawaii several times, Germany, Austria, Egypt, Israel, Greece, Holland, Australia, New Zealand, an African safari, London, Paris, Italy, Turkey, Spain, Ireland and several locations in Africa. We also earned wonderful cruises and national recognition for the work that we did.

What words of advice can you give to a consultant who really wants to grow their business?

If you are really interested in growing a business, join a company that you can get excited about. Talk to others about your choice before you commit and listen to others who already sell for that company. Ask questions, shop around...don't be shy! Shop around for a manager or leader who will help you get started and be there if you have questions.

Ask questions: Does the leader hold meetings? Offer promotions? Pass leads on to help you get started?

Don't just join a company with the first person you run into, as they may not be the best person to help you grow. Start slowly and be dedicated. Everyone wants to earn a trip or earn great commission their first year and many get discouraged when they don't.

Stay focused and keep trying. Don't sit around doing nothing. Keep in mind that you will get 20 people saying "no" before you get one who says "yes!" Ask 100 people and five will join your team or book a party. Encourage those five to get five more each and your business will be rolling.

If you truly have the want and desire to grow, you will. But you need to go out and get the business you want. It is not hard work, but it *is* work.

What do you want to achieve next?

There is not much more we can achieve professionally. We get tremendous joy from helping others grow their businesses, and we love watching people who have just earned their first trip or used their commission to purchase something special for their families.

We guess our goal today is to grow our current party plan business beyond the levels we previously enjoyed. We know this will take time and effort but we're patient. As long as we use the same business ethics as before, we'll eventually see the same results.

What do you enjoy most: Recruiting or sales? Why?

We run our business as a team. Sherry is holding parties and Chuck does most of the recruiting. We both get tremendous pleasure from what we do and really don't have a favorite. Both are equally important to be successful and we enjoy doing both.

What about bookings? How do you get bookings?

We have always found that bookings require a bit more work than holding the parties. It is a matter of asking people and then following up with them. Most bookings are obviously booked from the original party, so work with your original hostess and ask her to help you get some bookings. Many consultants make the mistake of never asking the hostess to help with their business.

Most party plan companies offer the hostess a great deal of free merchandise and we do not feel bad asking the hostess to encourage her friends to book parties. As customers place their orders, *ask* if they are interested in booking a party or if they would be interested in learning more about your company. If you don't ask, very few will offer.

If you notice a customer who would like to purchase several items and just can't afford it right now, she would be the perfect hostess (to get free merchandise). Maximum exposure and longevity is also important. Look around your city or town and get into as many local fairs and craft shows as possible. Yes, it will cost you a couple of dollars, but to make money, you must spend some first.

Have fliers in hand at fairs and talk about your business. Don't just let people walk by your booth. Invite them into your area and show them your favorite pieces. Maybe have an area set up to show what a hostess may get for holding a party.

Don't be shy. This is the type of business you need to go out and get. Don't wait for it to come to you.

How about your hostess? How do you coach her?

Hostess coaching is one of the most important parts of your party. The hostess, in many ways, is responsible for the success or failure of her party.

Encourage your hostess to share her enthusiasm and what she likes about your company. Ask her to let her family and friends know right away about the party, and to invite at least 25 people. Have her encourage each guest to bring a buddy along.

Encourage your hostess to send out invitations two weeks prior to the party, and ask her to follow up with each guest. Try to work with your hostess to get three to five outside orders (orders from people that cannot attend the party). Maybe offer to pay the hostess's shipping charges on products if she gets three orders prior to the party.

Work with your hostess so she is very familiar with the programs and how you plan on holding the party. Her enthusiasm about her party will lead to more people attending, which will lead to more sales and bookings!

Work with your hostess to create a "wish" list so you have a rough idea of what she would like to receive in free product from her party. Don't be afraid to encourage your hostess to get bookings for you. Be honest and let her know that your business depends on future bookings, and ask her to encourage her guests to book.

Which sales methods work best for you?

We are lucky that our current company offers fantastic products and the quality really enhances our sales. You must be knowledgeable, and that comes from being interested in your business. You must want to know about all the products, and get excited about what you are able to offer.

The tone of your voice, your excitement and knowledge of the products are your best assets at parties. Prior to your party, hostess coaching is very important. Be sure the hostess knows about all the programs and what is available. Encourage her to get several orders prior to the night of the party, and ask her if she knows anyone interested in booking a party from her party.

When you demonstrate at parties, it is important to show customers what the product does and the size and maybe suggest other items that would accent the original purchase. Create a dialogue and get customers talking about the product. Get people excited. Excitement breeds excitement.

Carry a current kit that shows a selection of products and ask your hostess if there is anything in particular she would like to see. If you have it, bring it. Bring enough merchandise and catalogues to your parties to set up a nice, professional display. Don't forget to leave a "consultant package" with the hostess, because she may know someone looking for a great part-time job.

After your party, follow up and let the hostess know how much you appreciate her letting you into her home and giving you the opportunity of sharing your company with her. Follow up again when the party order is delivered and build that relationship.

How do you develop leads for your business?

Many of our leads and new customers have come through holding parties. You will find that the party plan business is like a giant snowball. It starts with just one party (maybe your own), and the bookings help you get more parties. The more parties you hold, the more bookings you receive. Eventually, you could have more bookings than open dates. That is when you ask people to join your team and help them get started by passing a party or two their way.

Be sure you are with a great company that offers products your customers really want. Always have a catalog with you, just in case someone wants to see it. If we send a recruiting package to a potential new consultant and she does not want to join our team, maybe she will book a party instead.

What is your primary marketing method?

We have created a large mailing list through parties we have held over the years, and continuously call past hosts and customers to see if they would like to look at the newest catalogs when they become available.

We mail catalogs and send emails to our customers, letting them know about specials or promotions, and we always follow up. Once you start earning a decent living, mass advertising is a good source of generating business. It is also important to always talk about your business. It is the best free advertising you could ever get.

We also try to get into as many local craft shows and festivals as possible. They offer a great chance to show people your merchandise and, if you are allowed to buy product at a discounted price, pass the savings to the public. People will receive great products from your company at a good price and will remember the positives of your business when invited to a party. Craft shows or festivals cost about as much as an ad in the paper but work much better.

What advice can you give on joining local leads and business groups?

It is our experience that joining local or business groups does very little to help our business. We believe in focusing our business on holding parties and offering other people the opportunity to start their own business by joining our team. We are not really into joining groups or organizations.

Many times people can be so busy *running* their business that they are not *growing* their business. Stay focused and concentrate on what is helping you book parties and bring new people to your team.

What tips can you give about advertising? Has it worked for you?

It is very easy to think about advertising as simply placing an ad in the paper and waiting for the phone to ring. People who think this the only way to advertise are wasting their money. Sometimes the best advertising you can do is absolutely free: YOU are your best advertising, and talking to people about your business is free. Posting fliers on store bulletin boards is inexpensive. If possible, wear a pin or button that you have received from your business, or wear something you might sell. It creates conversation and gives you the opportunity to advertise your business.

When you set up a table at a craft show, summer fair, or church bazaar, have a banner made up with your company name. In many cases, the more merchandise you can get into the market, the more people will come to know who you are. Use company discounts and pass those savings on to customers at craft shows, just so people get to know who you are. Many stores create a "loss leader" (products you don't make money on, but that help you to get your name out there). We do the same thing.

I remember our previous company had beautiful green boxes for all their products. We sold a bunch of merchandise at local craft shows, but never gave out bags for customers to carry their purchases. Everyone walking around the shows saw all these people carrying green boxes. Eventually, people got curious and everyone started coming to our booth to see what was in all those green boxes!

Give some tips about inventory...does a new consultant need a lot?

It has always been our theory that the more merchandise you can bring to a party, the more people will be able to see and the more customers will purchase. We also realize there are some party plan companies that carry too many items, or items that are too heavy, which makes that impossible.

When you are doing crafts shows and local fairs, people love cash and carry. Bring merchandise you feel will sell. This will cover the cost of your booth *and* promote your business. (Most people will not just place an order at the craft show.)

Try to maintain as much product as you can, just in case someone needs an emergency gift or an item that is no longer available. When companies offer deep discounts on product for consultants, take advantage of what they offer.

The amount of product you keep as inventory is an individual question that each person must look at individually. Do you have the room? Can you afford a little inventory? It never hurts to have a few pieces on hand at your house or in the trunk of your car for when you are out.

What is your advice for recruiting and building a strong team? How do you manage them?

Holding parties and sharing the business opportunity is always your best bet. Hostesses hold parties because they love the product and since they know most of the programs through hostess coaching, they are also your best prospects. Always leave a recruiting package with your hostess and mention you have left some reading material just in case she knows of anyone looking for a great part-time job.

We stay in touch with all our customers through e-mail promotions and by sending out catalogues. Once your business starts to grow, place small ads in local papers and hold open houses at local hotels, churches, or at different halls. Invite everyone you know and ask them to bring a friend. Eventually you will be able to afford "cross country ads" that reach millions of people; that is when you really start receiving the phone calls.

Keep accurate records of who you sent recruiting packages to. It is especially important to follow up with a call. It is also important to work with the potential new consultants who are serious about joining your team. Don't waste your time leaving 10 messages to someone who does not return your call. Three calls are more than enough. Your third message should remind them of your number; your message should tell them that if they are ever interested, they should call you. This will create a want...if they are serious about joining your team.

Remember, out of 100 people, 5 five will join. If you spend all your time calling the same people, you will never get past your first 100 people. Get the maximum exposure for your business through fairs or local craft shows. The more people who see you and the product you offer, the better chance you have that someone will ask you "How did you get started?"

What are your most important learning experiences?

The most important learning experience is honesty and giving back to your business as much as it gives you. When we joined our first party plan company, back in 1991, our upline was in a different country and did not really offer us all the help we could have used. Times were different and there were reasons why, but still some days we felt alone.

When we had the opportunity to start leading people, we vowed they would never feel alone. As we grow our business, we make sure that we were always available and able to help. "I don't know" is not in our vocabulary, and we *always* make time for people on our team who are willing to grow and learn. After all, if our downline is successful, we are all successful. We also took the time and effort to learn our business inside out. We looked at the compensation plan and became experts on the programs. The more you know about the compensation programs, the easier you can build your team to maximize your commission.

Tips about motivation…how have you kept yourself motivated in order to rise to your professional level of success?

When we joined our first party plan company in 1991, our goal was to earn enough commission for dinner out once in awhile. It didn't take long to realize that adding new members to our team significantly raised our commission checks and our opportunity to earn fabulous trips.

As we grew, we tried to double our business every year and this worked out well. It also created a strong bond between the two of us and shaped a dream that someday we could quit our jobs and be completely self-employed.

At that time, our company was a U.S.-based company and we had to use a Canadian price list. We also had to manage all the importing and shipping throughout Canada. We could have easily quit and joined a Canadian company, but we were determined to accomplish something very few people in North America had ever done. We were determined that if everyone in Canada worked hard as a team and continued to grow, that eventually the company would recognize the growth and open a Canadian office.

In 1994, after the birth of our twins, Sherry quit her job. In 1995, with three small children, two car payments and a $160,000 mortgage, Chuck quit his job. It was a huge gamble but we knew that dedicating more time and effort to our business would pay off in the long run, and it has.

Our goals had changed from a few years earlier, and now our "want" was to maintain our family lifestyle by being self-employed. Over the years, as we started setting organizational sales records, our "wants" continuously changed. One year, we wanted to be #1 in sales and we focused on that. The next year we wanted to earn four trips, the following year was to earn enough to pay off our home. Finally, through the hard work of several hundred Canadian consultants, a Canadian office was finally established for that U.S.-based company and our sales continued to grow.

What advice can you offer to someone looking for a direct sales company to join?

Choose a company that offers unique items at a great price. This will help you book parties and that is the lifeline to future parties and success. Direct sales is extremely profitable if you work your business. Being a consultant and earning some extra money is also great but if you truly want to grow a huge profitable business it takes hard work, dedication and *time*.

What is your opinion about the future of direct sales?

Since 9/11 and the explosion of "big box" stores business has not grown at the same pace. In general, people will always like getting together with friends and family to have fun and share special times. We believe there will always be a need for party plan companies to share these special times.

Any final words?

Do what you enjoy doing and the money will follow. Take your time and your business will grow. Nothing happens overnight.

Our "want" today is to show our kids that through hard work, determination and perseverance you can accomplish anything you set your mind to. Today, as we venture out into different business areas with the experience we have, we know that honesty and determination will lead our way. We also know that our children are growing up in an environment where they see us working hard and receiving the benefits of running our own business. Even at their young ages they are already talking about being business owners and that puts a smile on our faces.

Your motivation and determination to succeed must come from your heart. Everyone is different and success is measured in many ways. Whether your goal is one party per week for some extra spending money, or two parties and one new team member every week to earn great commission or a trip, the decision is yours to make.

Nobody can grow your business for you…it is your will and determination that will help you reach your goals.

Leads group? It can be scary but it makes you come out of your shell! *Dawn R., Maryland*

NOTES:

Working From Home:
No License for Laundry

Admit it. You've looked at your phone and looked at the pile of laundry and the laundry won. Sometimes there are just about any other tasks that are more appealing than making calls and working your business. On certain days your zest is zapped and you cannot muster the motivation to even write the most cursory emails. These are the days you must plan for in advance.

It's easy to be motivated and energetic some days and be one step above couch potato on others. All days need a focus. If you are upbeat and able to knock out several phone calls, emails, and a newsletter mailing in just one day, you may take advantage of the energy and do just that. You may work an extra hour or two and get as much done as you can.

However, the very next day you may be tired and unfocused. Don't try to accomplish your high level tasks on these days. Use these days to do quiet work. Tasks like paying bills, filing, re-organizing, taking stock of inventory, etc. These are all necessary tasks for your business, but don't do them on days when you feel like you could take on the world.

How do you know what mood is coming next? It's not likely that every week you are given a pre-planned energy and motivation chart by your body. You just instinctively know that some days will be more business-oriented and productive than others. However, by developing a monthly plan of tasks you can stay on track and not get talked into mopping the floors, no matter how persuasive that mop can be.

Some days are going to require you summon energy due to pre-planned engagements you have. Some days will be taken over by personal and family reasons. Those days must be accounted for in your monthly plan. You may know that

Mondays are hard for you to get going, but on Tuesdays you are raring to go. Fridays may be for errands and kid's activities, but Wednesday and Thursday are free and clear for you to focus on your business. However your week is structured, you can develop an easy plan tailored to *your* needs.

Developing Your Monthly Business Focus

A Monthly Business Focus (MBF) is just what the name implies: A monthly focus for your business. It will help you focus on business building tasks. Instead of a scattershot "What should I do today?" program that many of us fall into, it will help you target certain duties for each week. It will break down larger goals into manageable smaller chunks.

First, you will need to commit to doing your MBF every month, or at least try it for six months. Get a clear calendar (a freebie from the bank or a print out from your computer works well). Be sure it has a nice square block for each day where you can write your tasks. We suggest you use a month-in-review type vs. a day-by-day calendar. It's easier to look at a whole month and see what is blocked out and where your energies are required.

Next, decide which days you already know are taken by other non-business commitments (family events, a root canal, a vacation, etc.). Block them off with a large X or similar symbol. Next, write in any business events you have planned (parties, conferences, meetings, etc.). You can then decide which days you know are typically low energy for you. These days should be noted "Admin." This means filing, paying bills, doing inventory, etc. These are "desk days" when you won't need a lot of energy and enthusiasm.

Marketing:

You will need to identify which day per week you will commit to marketing. You must do this at least one day every week (more if you have time). This doesn't mean holding sales parties or recruiting meetings. Marketing is for activities that include phone calls to prospects, doing newsletters, updating your website, developing promotions, doing email campaigns, etc. This day should be one that is free of other commitments and allows you to work for a block of at least four hours. Perhaps Tuesdays from 1:00 p.m. to 5:00 p.m. or Thursdays from 8:30 a.m. to 12:30 p.m. would work for you. Whatever you choose, block it out now and write "Marketing" on your calendar and at least three to four hours in one day of each week.

Sales:

Now you will identify a time for sales. Your sales day is an important day and must be allocated to a time of the week when you can focus and dedicate your efforts for a solid block of time (we recommend at least four hours). These activities are when you'll be concentrating on getting re-orders, following up with customers who have recently purchased products, up-selling, offering new seasonal items to existing customers, etc. *This is purely a time for product sales.*

Your sales day is your money-making day (exclusive of parties). You won't be contacting prospects for recruiting or writing your newsletter. This is only time for product sales. You can also be setting up parties or sales shows during these contacts since parties are a sales activity. This is the time when you concentrate on putting out as many seeds for sales as you can, whether they be re-orders, up-selling or booking a sales event. You want to bring in dollars during this time. You should focus on getting either a certain number of re-orders or up-sales (say a minimum of two re-orders or a dollar amount of at least $100.00). You should also focus on getting at least one booking during your sales time slot.

Of course you will be interrupted with phone calls and emergencies during these tasks but if you keep in mind how crucial they are for your success, you will be able to get back on task without too much trouble. For instance, on your marketing day you can set a goal to finish and send one newsletter promotion and on your sales day your goal would be to get $100.00 in re-orders, etc.).

For each day set a goal for the day and then commit to reaching it.

Bookings:

Now, how about bookings? If your business relies on sales events, you will need to spend time to work on getting bookings; this will be a crucial day for productivity. Although your marketing and sales days should both be times when you figure on getting at least one booking each, your booking day is when you must come through. While contacting prospects during the marketing phase and while getting re-orders you should always be asking for a booking. Be sure you have a carrot to offer (deep discounts, free gifts, etc.).

Janet, I really enjoyed meeting you at my (Company) party at Sarah's last week. I was calling to see how the XYZ products you bought were working for you? Do you have any questions about them?

You know, I would love to hold a party for you and your friends and family. I know you were interested in getting the (name high-priced product prospect had interest in) and I usually offer that at a 50% discount to my hostesses plus lots of other fun little treats. I have next Thursday evening open or maybe the following Saturday...

This type of conversation would be done during your booking slot. You have already sold this customer, now you need to obtain a booking. Or perhaps she was a potential recruit. Either way, this follow up call should be completed within a week from the initial sale and completed during the appropriate phase.

Recruiting:

This brings us to recruiting. If you are interested in building a team, you will need to focus on doing the tasks required for developing and managing recruits. You already know you should plant several seeds during your sales parties, but it is important to follow up with someone who seems especially interested but who didn't commit at the party.

Therefore, on your calendar name a day for recruiting and spend at least two to four hours on this. You may make phone calls, write emails or develop a special "Recruit this month and get a free product package!" mailer, etc. This time can also be used to manage an existing team. Have your meetings, training sessions, etc. on this day. Hold monthly team meetings on this day. This day is strictly for getting recruits and managing your team.

If possible, this day should also be used for physically meeting with anyone who wants to join or learn more about joining your company. Sometimes this is impossible due to people's varying schedules so even if you have to set a recruiting meeting for another time, you can use this time slot to make contacts, send follow-up emails, etc.

TIP: You should have at least five prospects on your immediate recruit list at all times. These are who you will focus on until you get a yes or no from them. When you cross one off, add another name to your list to keep it at five at all times. This will keep you focused. If a person says no, remember it may only mean no right now, so put them in a tickler file to present the opportunity to them again at a future time. For instance, if it's January and they say no, you may wish to present the opportunity to them again in June. A person's outlook can change dramatically in six months so always keep them in mind especially if they are a steady customer.

Final Note:

By now, your calendar is probably looking pretty full. You may have a full-time job or other full-time commitments. If so, mold this Monthly Business Focus to suit your schedule. If you cannot commit to four hours for marketing, commit to two, but do them consistently. If you work this MBF plan for at least 60 days, you'll find you have new habits that result in more sales, more bookings and more recruits.

This plan is not set in stone; however it should be followed as faithfully as possible during your first couple of months using it. After that, you will be able to identify which days are best suited for which tasks for you. If you find you have a high energy day that is slotted for administrative tasks, switch it around. Don't waste your energy and positive mood on low-energy tasks. Always use it to grow and create profit. These moods are better suited to taking rejection than low energy moods, so use them appropriately.

Finally, this should not be a daunting task. It should be simple, easy to follow and fit your particular lifestyle and needs. If you find you slot out these business tasks and complete them, you will not only feel like you have control over your business, you will notice measurable results. By contrast, if you don't complete the required tasks you may find yourself feeling guilty. If you find your original plan was too ambitious and you cannot devote as much time to each task slot as you thought, just reduce it until you find a program that not only works for you, but that you will work. That is the most important part of any plan.

❤

Interview:

Catherine Hughes

Company: Once Upon a Family
Title: Founding Director
Where: Tulsa, OK

Catherine is seller who strives to strike a balance between her home and professional life and from all accounts, she is very successful. She has provided a
straight-forward and user-friendly interview. Her relatively short time in business
and high team numbers show that she not only believes in her business and but
truly enjoys helping others join her in it.

How long have you been with your company?
Since 2003

How long have you been at your present level?
Over one year

How large is your sales team?
240+

Tell us about yourself

I've been married for 16 years and have three children. I enjoy horseback riding, water sports, anything outdoors.

Briefly describe your company (objective, services, products, etc.)

Once Upon a Family is a company that is designed to focus our efforts on the little things that we do each day. It also is a way to help teach family values and preserve family traditions. We have heirloom products that we sell, but our purpose is to give people the tools to enrich their lives. With over 240 on my team and over 50 directs, I have enjoyed watching my team achieve success. I have five Honorary Founders in my first generation!

What do you like best about your job?

I like that I am helping busy families focus on the important things in simple meaningful ways. Also, I can work this business whenever I want and I get paid for the effort that I put into my business.

Have you worked with any other direct sales companies?

No.

What principles have you followed to reach your current position with the company?

I have tried to stay consistent. Even if everything goes wrong, I just tell myself to take one step at a time.

What mistakes have you made?

Spending too much money on print advertising was one mistake. Also, thinking that all recruits were in it for the long term.

In your opinion, what does it really take to achieve your level of success?

Having drive and being persistent. Don't be a naysayer or complainer; it will bring you down.

What are your top sales tips?

1. Believe that you are sharing, *not* selling. Think of what our company has to offer and how *sharing* it with people will benefit them, not you.

2. Looking for ways to market other than a "party" situation.

3. Customer service.

What are your top recruiting tips? What helps you recruit?

1. Don't try to convince anyone.

2. Don't promise more than is realistic.

3. Let them know that you will be there for them.

What have you earned at the company (trips, cars, prizes, etc.)

Two cruises, one to Mexico and one to the Bahamas; a five-day, all expense paid trip to Cabo San Lucas; two "romantic weekends" with my husband; a three-day spa weekend.

What words of advice can you give to a consultant who really wants to grow their business?

Recruit, recruit, recruit.

What do you want to achieve next?

The level of Senior Director.

What do you enjoy most: Recruiting or sales? Why?

Recruiting. I enjoy learning from the people that I recruit.

How many parties should you hold each week for success?

I ideally have three or four a month.

What about bookings? How do you get bookings?

This is hard for me, but I would rather have one great show than 10 so-so shows.

How about your hostess? How do you coach her?

I would say this is a weakness of mine. I am working on this aspect. My advice would be to keep listening to company training until something sticks. The best advice I have received is this: If you walk to the door of your hostess's house for the party and feel like you are knocking on a stranger's door, you have not done your job before the party. You should be comfortable with your hostess before the party and feel like you are coming to the home of a friend.

How do you get most of your sales? (Internet, parties, one-on-one, etc.)

Most of my sales are one-on-one. I have a lot of repeat business from past customers.

How do you develop leads for your business?

Via the internet, friends, and by using other businesses to help mine.

What is your primary marketing method?

I use the internet. There are many sites that allow advertising and you can also join free groups which allow you to advertise your company.

What advice can you give on joining local leads and business groups?

I have not joined any.

What tips can you give about advertising? Has it worked for you?

Internet, yes. Print, no.

I feel that you *must* have a website to truly promote your business. A website is a 24/7 store for your company. Pay-per-click advertising is *not* something I have found to be effective. It never seems to pay in the end and there are ways to get your website ranked without this method. I have not researched the free options, but do you know that the longer you maintain your web address and people use it, the further up the rankings it will get?

Give some tips about inventory…does a new consultant need a lot?

No, my company doesn't encourage stocking inventory.

What is your advice for recruiting and building a strong team? How do you manage them?

We have weekly conference calls that anyone on the team can join in on. They are led by me and other leaders on our team. It is a great way to hold a long distance team together. There are many "free conference call" sites that you can sign up for. Type "free conference call" in on Google and it will give you many options. With these services, everybody pays for one long distance call.

What are your most important learning experiences?

Balance. It is hard to maintain an "all out" mode all the time. Your family will suffer and you will be exhausted. I was actually doing so much that I had too many leads and wasn't giving them the time that I needed to follow through with them. Break your business into specific goals and tasks and don't go further out than the year. See if you can hit monthly and weekly goals and the big ones will follow.

Tips about motivation…how have you kept yourself motivated in order to rise to your professional level of success?

I try to make a plan and stick to it. Connect with other people in the direct selling business and pick their brains. Everyone is going to have a down time, know that it will happen and that life will happen. Everyday is the first day of the rest of their business, so always look forward.

What are your top tips for a fun, profitable party?

Preparation and be one time! Have your things packed and ready to go; make sure as you unpack from one party to put things away so they are ready to go for the next one. Being rushed always stresses you out and you will not be relaxed walking into a group of people. Also, do what the guests are doing. If they are eating and offer you food, have a bit, either sitting on the floor or sit with them, etc.

What advice can you offer to someone looking for a direct sales company to join?

Find a company where you are passionate about the products. If you don't like what you are selling and want it yourself, you won't be able to sell.

What about strategies for success? In your opinion, what will help someone succeed in a direct sales business? Many start, but only a few will attain success while others drop out. Why?

To succeed in this business you can't look at a short-term streak. Some of the top girls on my team have been slow and steady rather than those who are stars for their first three months and then fade away. You need to know why you are doing the business. Is it financial or is it a hobby? Know too, that sometimes the people doing it as a hobby might become a business builder at some point. It is a matter of staying steady and looking three-to-five years out. Not everyone is comfortable doing that.

What about managing your day-to-day business? How do you stay focused on growing your business when laundry needs to be done or other distractions beckon?

I have to get up before the kids and get things done. I am a morning person, so for me, the early a.m. is the time to email and do paperwork. I also like to use a timer to keep me on track. You would be amazed at what you can accomplish in fifteen minutes!

Any final tips or ideas?

Stick with it! If you are not seeing the success that you want with your company, look to yourself. Don't look for excuses.

❧

Cats Not Invited

A few months ago I had a sales party for the sister of a friend I met at my daughter's school. She had some guests invited and was very polite on the phone although we had never met. I was excited to work the party and arrived a little early. I had only worked about a dozen parties at the time, so I was still fairly new at it and did not understand the value of hostess coaching.

Imagine my dismay when I walked in the door of her house and was hit with an overwhelming odor of cat urine and the sight of several cats running around. I like cats, but this was a bit much. The furniture was obviously the target of many scratching sessions from the cats; it was very shabby, but it was useable. The lighting was one small lamp in the corner and gave the room a dim yellow glow. I didn't know how I was going to make it through this party, much less actually sell or recruit!

My first impression was to cancel and get out of there and take a deep breath of fresh air in her driveway. However, she was nice and there were several guests expected, so I dug deep and went into emergency mode. I asked the woman if she could put some or all of the cats in another room, in case anyone had a problem with cats.

While she was doing that, I asked her for a small saucepot and some cinnamon, which thankfully she had on hand. I filled the pot halfway with water and poured a good amount of the spice in it and set it to simmer on the stove. I told her I often did this to give the home a warm, cozy feel. It was a bit of a lie, but I was stuck! I had remembered my grandmother doing this during the holidays and the memory luckily came to me that evening.

I then asked her if she had another lamp we could bring into the room for a little more light. As it was, the room looked lit by candlelight and guests would hardly be able to see my presentation much less my products and catalogs! She brought in a nice large lamp from her bedroom and set it on a corner table. It lit up the room dramatically.

By the time the guests arrived (only about 10 minutes later), I had the front door propped open for fresh air and the smell of cinnamon was starting to circle the room. The scent and the light was welcoming and warming and we had a nice evening and I even had a decent profitable party.

What did I learn? Several things:

- I learned how important it is to coach my hostess and explain the setting I will need to hold the party (no animals, good lighting, etc.) She will be an important link in getting her home ready if she knows what I expect.

- Be prepared: Carry candles, room scent or even a small bottle of cinnamon to use as an instant room freshener.

- Deal with it: The situation wasn't perfect, so what? The guests arrived, we had our party and I got some sales which may be re-orders or even recruits down the line.

- I learned that when things are less than ideal I need to think fast and work with what I have. You may not always have an "ideal" sales situation, but the bottom line is that your business is what you make it so you have to always try to make it good!

Interview:

Karen Clark

Karen Clark
Company: Story Time Felts
Title: Director of Consultant Development
Where: Rohnert Park, CA

Karen has the positive attitude and enthusiasm to propel her business forward. With an ever-growing team and a sincere belief in her products, she works toward goals for recruiting and sales. Her business building methods are both tried-and-true as well as creative and innovative. Her friendliness comes through and it is obvious why she is a top seller!

How long have you been with your company?
Since 1998

How long have you been at your present level?
Approximately one year

How large is your sales team?
106 currently active, counting directs and indirects; 44 of those are direct recruits.

Tell us about yourself

I am married and have two daughters and a baby boy: Fallon, who is 10, Alia who is 7, and Terry who is 1. My husband Greg and I live with the kids in the northern California wine country, where we grew up. I spend my free time spending time with our extended families, exploring the beaches and the redwoods and we enjoy camping. I volunteer at the girls' school and am active in the PTA. I am an elementary school teacher, currently taking time off to work my business full-time while my youngest is still small.

I spend time keeping up with my education by taking professional development courses and networking with active teachers. As a family, we go to the gym regularly, where the girls take fitness classes while Greg and I work out. I enjoy doing crafts with the kids and scrapbooking as well as reading, usually parenting or business books!

Briefly describe your company (objective, services, products, etc.)

We offer educational felt products, such as felt story sets, felt boards, puppets, masks and dolls to parent, educators, childcare providers and churches. We do this through home parties, on-site demonstrations, individual sales appointments, online sales and displays at public events, such as craft fairs or teaching conventions.

Our products are not available in stores and are unique in that they are washable, come with teaching ideas, include audio CDs of the stories put to music and are artistically detailed.

What do you like best about your job?

The part I enjoy the most about my job is the feeling that I am helping others enjoy a sense of accomplishment while bringing in an extra income for their families. Building a team has always been my favorite part because I love working with new consultants and watching them blossom.

Have you worked with any other direct sales companies?

No, this was my first direct sales venture! I had never considered a home-based business until I saw the products and knew I had to help spread the word!

What principles have you followed to reach your current position with the company?

1. Maximizing our exposure through the internet. We are a small company and through the internet I've been able to reach people in places that might not have otherwise ever discovered us.

2. Set clear goals. Through both company incentives and my own personal choice, I have always had a specific goal in mind, whether short or long-term. I make sure to do what it takes to work toward that goal every day.

3. Touch your business every day. It is easy, being at home, to let things slide. I make sure, even on lazy days, to do something productive toward my goals each day.

4. Persistence! I always knew I was meant to be a part of this company and that I would not quit!

5. Use available resources. There is always someone who can help you improve your business, whether it is from the company offices, your upline, past successful consultants or those in other companies. There are books and websites and newsletters just waiting for us to learn from.

What mistakes have you made?

It has been a challenge at times to rein in my enthusiasm and make sure I am meeting my family's needs first. Even though the company allows for flexibility, in the past it has been very easy to go overboard on the business because it is so much fun and I gain so much from it personally. Pacing myself and slotting in "me time" and "family time" can sometimes be a challenge.

I've also made some mistakes with not following up with leads, or not keeping in touch enough on a personal basis with my team as we've grown. I am sometimes overwhelmed and things or people slip through the cracks!

In your opinion, what does it really take to achieve your level of success?

It really takes putting in a lot of time and effort, and not giving up if you don't achieve your goals right away. Building a business takes time, and nothing happens without a little hard work! Sitting down and figuring out your goals, writing down a plan to achieve them, with specific tasks, is critical! Staying on top of all aspects of my business has been crucial.

What are your top sales tips?

1. Build a relationship with the customer. Find out what their needs are and treat them the way you'd like to be treated.

2. Don't be shy about finding out if the customer needs more than their initial order. Often, customers forget that they had another gift to shop for, or something they would need in the future, or they don't realize that we offer another product that goes great with the one they are ordering.

3. Always think of selling as sharing, not pushing! We have a great product I feel strongly about and believe in. How can I keep it a secret from everyone I meet? I have to share, accepting the yeses and the nos, but I have to at least share!

What are your top recruiting tips? What helps you recruit?

Build a relationship with your recruits. Find out what their needs are and treat them the way you'd like to be treated! Keep your focus on them and you cannot go wrong.

1. Don't be shy about finding out if the customer needs more than their initial order. Often, customers forget that they had another gift to shop for, or something they would need in the future, or they don't realize that we offer another product that goes great with the one they are ordering.

2. Be sure to always mention the business opportunity. You never know who would like an extra income or who knows someone who would love this business. Often, people don't even realize it is a business they can join. Share always!

3. Keep in touch with your team regularly through newsletters, email distribution lists, team meetings or chats and phone calls. Hearing from you on a regular basis is sometimes what keeps people going!

What have you earned at the company (trips, cars, prizes, etc.)

I have earned three cruises, three weekend getaway vacations, jewelry, product prizes and several recognition awards and certificates.

What words of advice can you give to a consultant who really wants to grow their business?

Do what you can to meet lots of people, and then establish a rapport with them so you can find out if your business fills a need for them. Do not persist with people who are not interested; accept the "no" and move on! There are lots and lots of people out there and the more of them you meet, the better your chances of meeting that future superstar. Encourage your downline to build downlines of their own and give them the support they need to be successful as team leaders themselves. Always keep up your own sales and be an example to your team, since more often than not they will do what you do! Be a great role model for them in every way!

What do you want to achieve next?

My goal for this year is to double my team to 200 active consultants. I will do this by offering incentives and encouragement to my existing downline and support them in growing their own team, and by continuing to spread the word to new prospects. I also have set a goal to sell at least $1,000 every month of the year, to set a good example for my team.

What do you enjoy most: Recruiting or sales? Why?

I have a lot of fun selling the product. I love talking about it and I am so passionate about the positive effect using our product has on children. Doing home parties and demonstrating at events is fun, however overall I'd have to say I enjoy recruiting the most. When working with prospective consultants, I get the best of both worlds. I get to share my love of the product *and* the benefits of the business opportunity while showing them that they can grow personally and professionally while adding to their income.

How many parties should you hold each week to build a profitable business?

I believe every consultant should strive to hold one party per week at the minimum to keep their business going. This means booking five or six for the month. If we do not have at least six to eight parties on the books coming up, it is time to get on the phone and get some more.

Having one party a week, whether you are a new start or a veteran, keeps you in touch with your customer and product. It also gives you more opportunities to create future business and sponsor team members. If someone has time in their schedule to do more than one a week, that's terrific! But by striving for at least one a week, everyone has an attainable goal.

What about bookings? How do you get bookings?

I talk about our home parties anywhere there are parents, teachers or childcare providers. I meet people through my own children's activities and schools or while we are out and about. I call up childcare providers and teachers and ask to show them our products, then explain how they can get some free. I also set up displays at local events with the goal of booking and recruiting. I emphasize that our parties are easy and fun and that children are welcome and I guarantee that everyone present will learn something!

How about your hostess? How do you coach her?

It is critical that a consultant keep in touch with her hostess and encourage her to keep in touch with her guests. I like to make my hostesses feel special by offering them extra incentives for things like holding her party on the original date, giving me her guest list early, personally calling all her guests, etc. In Story Time Felts, we are also encouraged to make the night before phone calls to introduce ourselves to the guests and find out what their specific needs are. I believe this really helps us get a good turnout, as the guests feel like the demonstration will be worthwhile.

How do you get most of your sales? (Internet, parties, one-on-one, etc.)

My sales are a combination of in-home parties and internet sales. Many of my internet sales are people who have already seen and experienced our products first-hand either through a home party or through samples I send through the mail. About 10% of my business is from making one-on-one appointments.

How do you develop leads for your business?

The same way I talked about getting bookings, plus internet exposure which helps me get individual customers throughout the U.S. Advertising my website and offering a free sample and mini catalog encourages visitors to stick around!

What is your primary marketing method?

Currently, most of my marketing is done through the internet. I am active on message boards and websites where our market clientele visit, such as parenting sites, childcare provider sites, teacher groups, etc. Posting on message boards or newsgroups, and then emailing prospects has been very successful for me.

What advice can you give on joining local leads and business groups?

I have some experience in the past with a local direct sales networking group and am in the process of starting one in my area. These can be great ways to get new ideas, share techniques and handouts and just get some local support from other experienced direct sellers. I have not participated in any other leads groups or business groups so far.

What tips can you give about advertising? Has it worked for you?

Passive advertising, such as newspaper or magazine ads and paid internet advertising usually does not work for me. The type of product we offer, since it is so unique, is very hard to understand and grasp without some explanation and a sample to feel and experience. Word-of-mouth and demonstrating in person have been the best methods for me. The internet marketing works well when I can explain fully what we are all about.

Give some tips about inventory…does a new consultant need a lot?

No. I have found that most people are perfectly happy to place orders since ours usually only take one week to arrive and we have no problems with backorders since the company makes the products on the spot, as ordered. Sometimes, when doing events such as craft fairs or holiday bazaars, it does help to have some cash-and-carry inventory since people like to shop for gifts that way, but it isn't necessary to be successful. I appreciate the fact that my company doesn't require us to carry an inventory.

What is your advice for recruiting and building a strong team? How do you manage them?

Keep good records and follow up with prospects. I have files on my computer where I keep the person's name and contact information and where I take notes each time I have contact with them. I then put in reminders on my computer to call or email them to follow up. When they join, I welcome them and follow up with an email or phone call after they've gotten their kit. I make sure they are invited to our online communities and chats and send them my newsletter.

What are your most important learning experiences?

Watching my upline, Lucy Brown, in action as she supported her team through newsletters, phone calls and being a great cheerleader in general has been the most valuable education! She set a great example for me, and encouraged me to reach my consultants through natural teaching moments, positive reinforcement, and steady contact.

Tips about motivation...how have you kept yourself motivated in order to rise to your professional level of success?

All I have to do is look at my family and I am motivated! Staying home with my children has been such a reward and even when I am teaching, I am able to only teach part-time, thanks to this business. Setting concrete goals such as paying for something I want but that wouldn't normally be in the family's budget helps too, such as new carpeting or a trip. I make notes to myself and leave them around the office and on the fridge to keep me inspired!

What are your top tips for a fun, profitable party?

You will sell more, book more, and recruit more if your parties are simple and fun! Have some sort of ice breaker to get all the guests involved. Get them laughing and they will buy, book and recruit!

What advice can you offer to someone looking for a direct sales company to join?

Look for something that fits into your lifestyle. For me, I needed something that I could involve my children in or have daytime parties and bring them along. It is also important to find a company that is established, has a generous compensation and hostess plan and lots of support for their consultants.

What about strategies for success? In your opinion, what will help someone succeed in a direct sales business? Many start, but only a few will attain success while others drop out. Why?

The key is PERSEVERENCE. Most people who fail give up just before their businesses start taking off! It takes at least a year to get established and another year to really take off! Work your business consistently and do not give up!

What about managing your day-to-day business? How do you stay focused on growing your business when laundry needs to be done or other distractions beckon?

Develop routines to make your days go smoothly. Trim your "to do" list to "must do's" and let the rest go. Your business should be toward the top of your list! If you have routines established for the day-to-day duties, when something comes up you are better able to handle it. Touch your business every day, no matter what, in some way.

Any final tips or ideas?

Be sure to take advantage of all of the resources out there from your company and the direct sales community. There is a lot of knowledge and expertise you can learn from, whether you are just starting or well established! Best of luck!

What keeps me motivated? I have pictures up in my office of all the things I want!
Lora G., Massachusetts

<u>NOTES:</u>

Interview:

Jaye Adams

Company: Daisy Blue Naturals
Title: Senior Leader
Where: Austin, MN

Jaye represents a company whose growth is undeniably due in part to Jaye's stellar efforts. Her passion for her business and the products she represents really comes through. Her get-it-done approach helps you understand why Jaye is a success!

How long have you been with your company?

Since 2001

How long have you been at your present level?

1+ year

How large is your sales team?

145+

Tell us about yourself

I live in Minnesota. I have been married to my husband, Bruce, for 17 years. We have four kids between us and nine grandchildren. My hobbies include walking, country music, fishing and relaxing.

Briefly describe your company (objective, services, products, etc.)

My company is Daisy Blue Naturals, which is based out of Albert Lea, MN. Our objective is to provide truly all-natural body and household products as an alternative to products that have harsh chemicals and preservatives. We have a variety of oils and lotions, baby, men laundry, facial, soaps, butters, feet, hand, and healing oils available.

What do you like best about your job?

Being in from the beginning and seeing the changes that only make us better. I was the 6th consultant to sign up with Daisy Blue and I have loved it from the beginning.

Have you worked with any other direct sales companies?

I was with a food company for one year but it was way too much work and preparation.

What principles have you followed to reach your current position with the company?

I believe passion for your product is the leading reason a person is successful with any home-based company. If you love your products and what they stand for, that enthusiasm shows. I also know my opinion counts in my company. I feel like I can suggest things and they really listen to me. You also have to spend the time. I personally won't sell anything that isn't consumable so that means you have to get your name out there. I spent a lot of time at craft shows, expos, etc. to make a name for myself. I still do that, but not as much. I also try to make my customers feel special and important.

What mistakes have you made?

My biggest mistake is follow-up. I'm not really good at picking up the phone and following up with customers on a monthly basis.

In your opinion, what does it really take to achieve your level of success?

Passion for your product, persistence and hard work.

What are your top sales tips?

1. Knowledge of your product.
2. Having a full kit for testing (you can't sell what they can't try.)
3. Offering additions like a dish with the soap, or a peppermint foot butter with the crystals they bought.

My best sales method is letting them try our products. They get to do a hand scrub when they first get to my party and then they get to soak their feet and pamper themselves after that. Women (and men) need that, don't they?

In building your business and team, what are your most important learning experiences?

I learned that I can't be and do everything for every person in my downline and work with what they want to build a strong business. Sometimes what I want for someone isn't what they want and I have to respect where they are in life. I have also learned that if you want something bad enough, you can have it by hard work and drive. This is a business that you have to go after. It won't come to you. Those who are self-motivated are the most successful.

What are your top recruiting tips? What helps you recruit?

1. Talk about what your company offers for consultants.
2. Getting a NO is OK.
3. Be prompt about follow-up with someone who is interested in your company.

Getting a new consultant set up with what she needs to get started is a good tip. I have made up a lot of helpful tools for the new consultant like price lists, my outline of a party, a benefit sheet so she knows what our products do for you, etc. I will also do her first show for her to help her have a full kit (you can't sell what you don't have).

What have you earned at the company (trips, cars, prizes, etc.)

We are a new company so we don't have any big "prizes" yet. I have earned two free trips and many little things along the way.

What words of advice can you give to a consultant who really wants to grow their business?

Don't be afraid of "no." You have to be willing to talk to everyone about your company and products. I find it so easy to do because I know what our products do for people and how I can help them feel better.

What do you want to achieve next?

I want to be our company's first Director. I have met all of my prior goals like top sales, top recruiting, top team sales, etc. so that's next on my list. We'll see what happens!

What do you enjoy most: Recruiting or sales? Why?

I like selling. I have a lot more control over myself and can get out and sell my products with no problem. I love what I do!

How many parties should you hold each week?

Two; I think everyone can handle that on a weekly basis.

What about bookings? How do you get bookings?

Ask, ask, ask! You won't get them any other way!

How about your hostess? How do you coach her?

Send out invites, call ahead of time and set them up for a good show. Show enthusiasm about what they are going to earn free, give them samples for those who cannot attend and help them be successful. It's more about what's in it for them than what's in it for me. Concentrate on them (your hostess) and you will both be successful.

How do you get most of your sales? (Internet, parties, one-on-one, etc.)

Parties. I have also built a great re-order business.

How do you develop leads for your business?

By doing lots of parties, I have never gotten a new customer by sitting at home.

What is your primary marketing method?

Parties, craft shows, referrals. My company is headquartered in my area, so more people have heard about us where I live.

What advice can you give on joining local leads and business groups?

I suggest joining anything that can help your business grow.

What tips can you give about advertising? Has it worked for you?

I usually don't have very good luck with advertising but I do get out there personally every chance I get. I make sure I'm at every event I'm invited to or can get into. Our products have to be experienced to be appreciated.

Give some tips about inventory…does a new consultant need a lot?

No. Yes, a consultant should have a full kit, but cash-and-carry, no. Our company has a two-day turnaround so on-hand inventory isn't a big deal. I do cash-and-carry now because women love to take their products home with them but it took me a long time to build that up and it's not necessary. It's only because I choose to do that.

What is your advice for recruiting and building a strong team? How do you manage them?

You must recruit if you are going to be successful long term. I am learning skills on training my first line and new recruits so in turn they can train their team. What works for one leader may not work for another. Keeping in touch with those that want a strong, successful business is my best piece of advice.

Tips about motivation…how have you kept yourself motivated in order to rise to your professional level of success?

I love my products, my company, the owner, and the vision of where we are going as a team.

What are your top tips for a fun, profitable party?

Keep it short, make each person feel special, and suggest ad-on items for additional sales. Changing things up for repeat hostesses is important to make each party fun and worth coming to.

What advice can you offer to someone looking for a direct sales company to join?

Find a company that offers products that you are passionate about. Don't join a team just because of the compensation plan.

What about strategies for success? In your opinion, what will help someone succeed in a direct sales business? Many start, but only a few will attain success while others drop out. Why?

People in this business usually fail because they really never got started in the first place. If you are going to join a direct sales company, start it right away. Get the knowledge you need from your upline and get started. And, remember, this is *your* business and it will succeed or fail by how you take care of it. Nobody will do it for you.

What about managing your day-to-day business? How do you stay focused on growing your business when laundry needs to be done or other distractions beckon?

You need to find a balance in your life to fit it all in. I have never had trouble staying focused because I knew where I wanted to go with this. I admit, sometimes I get lazy, but setting goals helps you know where you're going and helps you get there. It also helps to have support of your family to get it all done. Everyone gets rewards when I am successful. That keeps them motivated as well.

❤

Regarding hostess coaching: Keep in *constant* contact with the hostess. It's *very* important to keep her enthusiasm up. Book in close to avoid cancellations.
Lorian R., Florida

NOTES:

What's Your Plan?

Excerpt from PUMP News Guides

Asking new business owners if they have a business plan usually elicits a roll of the eyes or a groan. *"Who has time to put together a business plan? Besides I'm just a small home-based business. I don't need a business plan."* Sure you do! The following is a very simple plan you can set up in a short time. Once you get it on paper it's easier to stick to it.

A business plan is a necessity. However, putting together a strategic and easy-to-follow plan doesn't need to take more than an hour or so. One hour…isn't that a small amount of time to invest in growing your business? Especially when you consider studies show that those who do have a plan far exceed in growth those who don't?

Putting together a basic business plan only requires thoughtful response to a few questions. You don't need executive summaries, strategic operations outlines, etc. The questions can be simple. They can be varied and worded differently, but essentially the questions are similar:

- **What is your business?** This question is easy to answer. Describe your business, products, etc.

- **What is unique about you and your business?** This one may be a little tougher. You may be in a one-of-a-kind business or a representative for a well-known company with thousands of other reps. Either way, you and you alone bring something different and unique to your business. What will you do that's a little different? This can be a terrific question to help you build your marketing strategy down the road. Find what it is that you will offer that's unique and sets you apart.

- **Who is your ideal customer?** This is a great question to help you define to whom and where you will market your business. Write down a couple of descriptions of your ideal customers. This will tell you a lot about where you might find them and how you can approach them. (i.e. are they women, men, parents, working professionals, health enthusiasts, etc.?)

- **What is your focus?** Are you a product sales company or do you want to focus on providing services? Do you want to do both, and if so, how will you do this? What is your primary goal? Thinking about this may give you some surprising answers. You may feel you want to sell a lot and earn a lot of money, but after consideration you decide your primary goal is to help people, provide education and tools for their life. Your goal would be likely to recruit and help mentor and educate your team more than focusing on sales.

- **What is your monthly sales goal?** What are your goals now, 6 and 12 months from now? Do you want to sell $1,000 a month now, $2,000 a month in 6 months and $5,000 in 12 months? Those are good goals, but are they realistic? Do you know what it will take to reach them? Can you do what it takes? Be honest with yourself. If not, set realistic goals that you can attain. Set your goals high enough where you feel challenged, but not so high that you will feel defeated. Nothing will discourage you faster than not reaching your goals and giving up. Let some people close to you know your goals. If you tell people you plan to succeed, it is harder to give up.

- **What are your three primary methods to market your business?** Will you do phone calls, mailings and a web site? Or perhaps you prefer media releases, working your circle of influence and leaving brochures with local retailers. There are many ways to market effectively. Choose three which *you know you will do.* If you know you'll never write a release or do cold-calls, don't list them. Choose the ones you know you will and can do consistently.

- **How long will you work on your business each day?** Set up a schedule you will be able to follow. If you can only work your business every Tuesday and Thursday for one hour between 7 and 8 p.m., note this in your plan. Then stick to it. If you can devote more time, do so. The most important part of this is to really stick to that schedule. You won't have a clock to punch or a boss to answer to, so it must be up to you.

If you really want to stick to your schedule, put signs up around your house to let everyone know where you'll be at your specified times. Let them know you won't be disturbed...you are working! Lock your office door and turn off the TV, phone, etc. If you want to make your business work, you must work at it.

Sticking to a schedule will help. Don't try to fit work in whenever you have a few minutes. You can always add time to your regular schedule throughout the week, if necessary.

Sit down and write out your answers. Post them above your desk. Look at them often to stay on track. These questions will give you a basic roadmap to get you started. If you can set up a schedule for one month to do the tasks you have listed, you will find your business develops a solid base within 90 days. If you can follow this program for just a few months, you will certainly be able to achieve your goals.

❤

Interview:

Paul Lauderdale

Company: Synergy Worldwide
Title: Independent Distributor
Where: Dallas, TX

Straight-forward and committed to success are phrases that may best describe Paul. After learning more about his business background, it becomes clear as to why he has had success on a consistent basis. Paul finds something that works and sticks with it. Most importantly, he takes those findings and shares them with others. His staggering team numbers make it easy to understand why he has found "his home" in the world of direct sales.

How long have you been with your company?

Since 2002

How long have you been at your present level?

Over 6 months

How large is your sales team?

25000+

Tell us about yourself

I founded a Dallas, TX-based company in the late 1980s that became the 53rd fastest growing privately held business in the US by 1992. I then sold the business and retired in 2000 at the age of 42. I began to look for a new opportunity and was contacted by my best friend from childhood, Keith. Keith had retired from a well-known skincare company as Sr. V.P., Secretary of the Board and original shareholder. He told me about a company called Synergy Worldwide. I currently own three businesses: commercial real estate, an internet-driven specialty equipment company and a Synergy Worldwide distributorship.

Briefly describe your company (objective, services, products, etc.)

Synergy offers health, wealth and wisdom by manufacturing and distributing cutting-edge products that are consumable, emotional and proprietary.

What do you like best about your job?

The international opportunity it offers and helping others.

Have you worked with any other direct sales companies?

This is my first and last direct sales experience.

What principles have you followed to reach your current position with the company?

Hard work, working smart, working as a team and a little luck!

What mistakes have you made?

In the beginning, I recruited by telling people that they were going to make a lot of money. As I began to understand the business I realized the necessity to work hard, work smart as a team and that it takes two to three years to build a business. Most millionaires in the industry have five to seven years' experience.

In your opinion, what does it really take to achieve your level of success?

There are several factors. In addition to the above principles I listed you need patience, persistence, and a strong team. I am sponsored by one of the top people in the industry, Keith Halls. I am also coached by two of the top people in the industry, John Fuhrman and Seth Mulder.

What are your top sales tips?

1. Keep your belief at the highest possible level

2. Be honest, open, and ethical

3. Never give up

What are your top recruiting tips? What helps you recruit?

The best way to recruit is person-to-person. I have spent thousands on internet recruiting, job fairs, etc…At the end of the day, person-to-person works best. Be as enthusiastic as possible about your program. Always be open, honest, and ethical. Inform your prospects without being phony or high pressure.

Also, work smart and focus on:

1. People that are hungry for an opportunity
2. People that have networking experience
3. People that have success and leadership skills
4. People with international contacts

What words of advice can you give to a consultant who really wants to grow their business?

Find a good company. Find a good team. Find a good coach. Make a plan and work your plan…BE PATIENT.

What do you want to achieve next?

Besides the obvious, top level in Synergy Worldwide, I have team members that I am investing time and effort in to help them achieve their dreams

What do you enjoy most: Recruiting or sales? Why?

Recruiting. It is a multi-faceted process. In addition to bringing in new members, the process also trains your new and existing members. This process is the lifeblood of any MLM company.

How many parties should you hold each week?

Generally, one event per week for the aggressive business builder. Quarterly, they should attend a major company event…plus the annual convention.

What about bookings? How do you get bookings?

I utilize a variety of methods. The tools and techniques that you use in this business are numerous and take many years to master. My advice is to find what *works* and do this as often as possible.

How about your hostess? How do you coach her?

My advice to the developing leader or hostess is to help your people make money as quickly as possible.

How do you get most of your sales? (Internet, parties, one-on-one, etc.)

Personal referrals.

How do you develop leads for your business?

1. Person-to-Person

2. Internet Ads

3. Local Newspaper Ads

4. Purchased Leads

5. Associations, Friends, etc....

What is your primary marketing method?

There are many methods used in my international group. We use all of the above and many more. I really like person-to-person.

What advice can you give on joining local leads and business groups?

Only do this if you are genuinely interested in the local group. There is enough superficial recruiting that already goes on in this industry. If you are really interested in a particular organization's activities, then this method can be effective.

What tips can you give about advertising? Has it worked for you?

Spend as little money as possible...measure your results from a small sample before committing to more funds.

Give some tips about inventory...does a new consultant need a lot?

If your opportunity is genuine, very little inventory will be necessary. International markets are different and often require various distribution points.

What is your advice for recruiting and building a strong team? How do you manage them?

Keep in touch weekly with the key leadership.

What are your most important learning experiences?

Again…work hard, work smart, work as a team…and be patient and persistent.

Tips about motivation…how have you kept yourself motivated in order to rise to your professional level of success?

Other books as expressed in our library on http://www.synergypower.info. And (to remember) the #1 reason "why I joined in the first place." Write this down and review it daily as it will help you through the toughest times.

What are your top tips for a fun, profitable party/sales event?

Be early, upbeat, keep the event exciting and professional; remember that your excitement about the program will spread.

What advice can you offer to someone looking for a direct sales company to join?

Make sure they are financially stable, understand the industry and have a committed and ethical management team.

What about strategies for success? In your opinion, what will help someone succeed in a direct sales business? Many start, but only a few will attain success while others drop out. Why?

Most people are not patient and expect success right away. I believe that if you give people the *long-term vision* in the beginning, the retention rate will be much higher. If you can help them make a few hundred dollars in the first few months, they will more than likely stay with the program for a couple of years.

What about managing your day-to-day business? How do you stay focused on growing your business when laundry needs to be done or other distractions beckon?

I continually re-shuffle priorities.

Any final tips or ideas?

Feel free to call or contact me anytime for additional comments or help. As a professional in the industry; I can always take a few minutes to help professional networkers.

Don't spend a lot of money on advertising while your business is still small. Rely on person-to-person contact. It's the most important thing. *Kim R., Utah*

<u>NOTES:</u>

Interview:

Suzanne Bressler

Company: Avon Products, Inc.
Title: Executive Unit Leader
Where: Summerdale, PA

Ms. Bressler obviously loves her career and feels she's made the right choice. She says she markets herself at every opportunity, but does not pressure friends and family to become a part of Avon. She has a good sense of her long-term goals. Ms. Bressler seeks out women who are serious about a direct sales career so as not to waste her own time or that of her recruits.

How long have you been with your company?
Since 1990

How long have you been at your present level?
2+ years

How large is your sales team?
141+

Tell us about yourself
I've been married 29 years and have two children. I started with Avon because I wanted to have flexibility with my church duties. I'm involved with ministry. My hobbies include reading and going out on our boat. The boat was a reward we gave ourselves because of my success with Avon. We set that as a goal and were excited to have reached it.

Briefly describe your company (objective, services, products, etc.)

Avon is the largest cosmetic company in world. It is touted as "*The* company for women." They support a lot of events and programs for women.

What do you like best about your job?

I like the flexibility and excitement. I also enjoy the people element. No two days are the same. It's great seeing others reach their goals. Everyone brings new ideas and approaches. I enjoy the benefits of that.

Have you worked with any other direct sales companies?

No

What principles have you followed to reach your current position with the company?

1) Persistence

2) Patience

3) Talk to three women a day

I steadily look for new customers and offer them the opportunity. I've always written out my goals and worked toward them. Recently I found an old planner with goals written down. I had forgotten them, but later realized I reached them. And of course, I provide excellent customer service.

What mistakes have you made?

I didn't start leadership as soon as it was offered. Prior to ten years ago, Avon did not emphasize leadership or teams, just sales. I got involved with leadership five years ago. I really wish I'd done it earlier.

In your opinion, what does it really take to achieve your level of success?

Determination and patience. Juggling personal life and business life. Some days are not interesting and some people aren't interested. It's important to be able to bounce back.

What are your top sales tips?

I use demos, offer two week free trial on new products. I also encourage repeat business by excellent customer service. Also, bundling—selling several products that go together. I like add-on sales like lip liner with lipstick, etc.

What are your top recruiting tips? What helps you recruit?

I take a very subtle approach with friends. I did not approach friends and family first. I didn't try to recruit friends because I did not want them to feel used. It has worked out well because they've made the decision to do it and they've been solid team members. Plus:

- Advertise always; put personal stickers on brochures.
- Leave brochures everywhere.
- Participate in events like craft shows and charity events to meet new people.

What have you earned at the company (trips, cars, prizes, etc.)

A diamond necklace and trophies. Our team won all of the division trophies for leadership.

What words of advice can you give to a consultant who really wants to grow their business?

Make definite plans on what you are going to do each week, have a schedule that you stick to and make progress everyday.

What do you want to achieve next?

I want to reach senior Executive Unit Leader. That would entitle me to a car allowance. I can pick any vehicle I want up to $800 a month; Avon covers it. I need more team members who are building solid teams. I'm downsizing my sales business to focus on team building. I'm making plans to delegate 2/3 of my customers to my downline to spend time training, recruiting and motivating. I hope I've trained my team well enough to offer the same quality service to my customers that I've offered. It's a better money opportunity for me to focus on team building right now.

What do you enjoy most: Recruiting or sales? Why?

Recruiting because I get excited about finding new people and seeing their excitement and progress. A couple of my team members have had enough money to buy a house because of the extra $$$ earned from Avon. They kept their regular jobs, but supplemented their income with their Avon business.

What about bookings? How do you get bookings?

I only do grand openings for new reps. I don't really do the house parties. I chose Avon because I did not want to do parties and chase down hostesses.

How do you get most of your sales? (Internet, parties, one-on-one, etc.)

Cold calls on offices, door-to-door, craft shows and festivals.

How do you develop leads for your business?

I do door-to-door sales. Avon is non-threatening and people love it. Lately, I've done more with businesses. I just walk in and ask if they currently have an Avon person. I leave catalogs; they fax and email their orders. I place-orders, deliver in two weeks, they pay, and that's it. No stress involved.

What is your primary marketing method?

I didn't have any sales with direct mailings. Cold calling at offices has worked well for me.

What advice can you give on joining local leads and business groups?

I have never joined any groups. My church work keeps me busy.

What tips can you give about advertising? Has it worked for you?

Yes, I use a little bit of advertising. Make sure you set a budget for advertising. Be consistent. You have to do it (advertise) at least a month straight to get real results.

Give some tips about inventory…does a new consultant need a lot?

No, a new consultant does not need a lot of inventory. I encourage my reps to learn what their customers will want first. Once they have a handle on their business, they can order inventory. We get our products in a few days after ordering. I teach them that they don't need to get into debt with Avon.

What recruiting methods work best for you?

Avon teaches us "The Power of Three." Talking to everyone is best including waitresses, patients in doctor's office, theater ticket collector, etc. Make sure you talk to *at least* three women a day. Stickers on brochures have yielded quite a few team members. Leaving brochures everywhere has gotten me calls that lead to team members.

Tips about recruiting…what have you found that works best?

Low pressure, high follow-up. I let them decide without manipulation then I follow up every now and again to see if they are interested. I end up with people who want to do it.

What is your advice for recruiting and building a strong team? How do you manage them?

Regular communication is important. Working together helps build our relationship as we increase sales. Our downline manager program on the Avon website helps us to track progress and determine who needs help.

What are your most important learning experiences?

I learned to offer every new rep the opportunity to build her team right away. Initially I waited until they built their business and then offered it. I should have been doing that all along. It makes them excited and they transmit that to their friends and build a team. Don't prejudge who will stick with it/who has potential. The recruit in front of me may not stick it out, but may lead me to someone wonderful who will stick it out.

Tips about motivation…how have you kept yourself motivated in order to rise to your professional level of success?

I read a lot: Books on network marketing, sales, selling, motivation. I still get excited by doing it. Getting a new customer or recruit is exciting. That keeps me motivated.

What advice can you offer to someone looking for a direct sales company to join?

If you're just starting out don't be drawn to companies that need thousands of dollars in start-up fees and inventory. An Avon career can begin with just $5-$15.

What about strategies for success? In your opinion, what will help someone succeed in a direct sales business? Many start, but only a few will attain success while others drop out. Why?

Keeping focused on dreams and goals is paramount. Many lose sight of their long-term goals and let themselves get distracted by minor annoyances.

What about managing your day-to-day business? How do you stay focused on growing your business when laundry needs to be done or other distractions beckon?

That can be challenging. I try to stick to a schedule so that my other priorities (my faith and family) are not neglected.

Any final tips or ideas?

Don't be discouraged by those who quit. Keep meeting people and you'll find the ones who will work with you to achieve great success for everyone. Find joy in watching new reps blossom.

Create a Referral Rainfall!

Does this sound familiar?

1. You have customers.

2. Your customers enjoy your product or service.

3. You're frustrated because, even though your customers know you and like your products and services, they DON'T TELL anybody about how good you are.

Like referrals? Everybody does. They are a warm lead. A lead that says "someone I know and trust recommended you." That almost helps to create a sale without anything else. However, sometimes getting referrals is sometimes awkward. Asking your satisfied customers is easy—as long as you remember to do it.

To ensure you don't forget, develop a flier that goes to everyone who places an order. Let them know how much you appreciate referrals. Ask them to email you the name, address, and phone/email of three people. If they do, send them a free gift. After a customer orders, you can follow up a few days later to ask how the products are performing, do they have any questions, etc.? At this time, ask your *new* customer for a few referrals.

> *I went to a new salon for a haircut. I really liked the service and was pleased. But what really impressed me was that a few days later I received a follow-up phone call to be sure I was happy with my haircut! I let them know I was and they asked me to send them a referral of any friends who may need a new salon. I ended up sending them lots of business—because of the great haircut and the great follow-up call!*

Wouldn't it be amazing if every service provider contacted you after the service to see if you were pleased, if you liked the products you purchased, had any questions, etc.? Providing follow-ups consistently will make you remembered and treasured as a product and service provider.

VIP Cards

Develop a discount card. Make it a VIP (Very Important Person) card. Print on it that you offer a 20% discount to holders of the card. Give them out to all your customers and include a few extra for them to give to others.

You can even team up with another vendor or two or whose name and logo you can include on the back. You will each offer these cards to all your customers (teaming up with other vendors gives you double or triple the customers for potential distribution). Each seller can share a portion of the cost of developing the card.

It needn't be expensive to produce. You can make them on your computer on pull-apart business cards, or you can have them professionally designed and printed. Just be sure the final result is professional, elegant (after all, VIPs deserve elegance), and something you are proud to distribute.

Complementary Business Referrals

Make a list of people/businesses that sell complimentary products and services to your own product or service. Ask them to be involved in your VIP card program or ask them to send you referrals for your business. Be sure to let them know you will do the same.

To make this system more effective, develop a referral card, coupon or flier for them to hand out to their customers. You should include their logo/name on it as well as your own. This does two things: It will help promote them (it has their name/logo on it) and it will let you know where the referral is coming from. Be sure to always ask your new customers how they heard of you. If they mention this flier ask what other company is listed on it. Track who is sending you referrals and be sure to send them referrals consistently.

Example:

You are ABC Cosmetics and you partner with DEF Candles. You develop a flier with a promo from each of you and with each of your names. Both you and DEF Candles give this flier out to customers, etc. When a new customer calls you, ask how they heard of you. If they reply that they have a flier from DEF Candles, then you know DEF Candles is where the referral came from. Send DEF Candles a thank you, a little gift or a certificate. And be sure to send them referrals, too!

Freebies/Raffles

Here is an easy one: Give your products or services away (or significant discounts on your products or services) in local raffles. The raffle can benefit a worthy local cause. If you can offer something of value to the winner, you can not only add the person to your customer list, you can up-sell them on other products and future items. You may not make money on the first contact (as it was a free item give-away) but you may make a lifelong customer or recruit.

Thank You Notes

This system will not only bring you referrals, but it will also create a lot of good-will. A story goes that when a famous royal died a close associate of hers was inter-viewed and revealed that she always carried a set of "royal" thank you notes. Every time she met with someone she would remember their names and as soon as she got in her car she would write a short thank you note to them. The people cher-ished the thank you notes they received from her.

Even if you are not a Princess and cannot sit in the back of a limo and write thank you notes after meeting someone, you can write them daily or weekly. At the end of the day or week, make it your task: Write and send thank you notes for anyone you met, new prospects, and cherished customers. If you make it a regular task, it will work as a marketing tool (to keep you in their thoughts), as well as a service tool. By doing it regularly it will keep from becoming an overwhelming task.

Each of these referral tactics are **systems**. They motivate others to generate refer-rals for you. The best thing you can do to excite your referral partners is to get them to experience your product or services themselves. Then they can talk about it with first-hand knowledge. It will not only make you more credible to others but once they've experienced the benefits of what you have to offer, they will be more excited to tell others about it.

If you use these systems professionally and consistently, referrals can soon be your best source of new customers.

Interview:

Eileen Blackburn

Company: Premier Designs High Fashion Jewelry
Title: Two-Diamond Designer
Where: O'Fallon, IL

Eileen is a busy, on-the-go professional with a dedicated focus on her business. By believing in her company, its vision and the rewards it gives her, she has been able to build her business with a strong relationship-centered team.

How long have you been with your company?
I started with my company in July 1998

How long have you been at your present level?
9 months

How large is your sales team?
50+

Tell us about yourself
I am married with one daughter. I am a retired U.S. Air Force military officer and hold a post graduate degree. I enjoy travel, reading, walking, roller coasters, cooking, dining out (when I'm tired of cooking), and coaching!

Briefly describe your company (objective, services, products, etc.)

We sell high fashion jewelry through a direct sales environment, i.e. home shows, corporate image impact seminars, bridal jewelry shows, fundraisers, and catalog shows. Our Biblically-based company celebrated its 20th anniversary as of 2005. We were founded to help moms stay home with their children, to minister single parents financially, to provide additional income for Christian workers, and to support missions in America and around the world. Our marketing plan states we exist to honor God and to serve people. In fact, we are a people-driven company, not a profit-driven company, and we are also a debt-free company!

What do you like best about your job?

I like the flexibility it offers me to be available to my family.

Have you worked with any other direct sales companies?

Yes, I was with a skincare/cosmetics direct sales company. I wish I had known about Premier Designs High Fashion Jewelry at that time—I would have chosen this company instead because I believe in my heart that we have the best marketing plan and hostess plan out of all the other direct sales companies out there.

What principles have you followed to reach your current position with the company?

I believe in honoring God, providing consistency, and having a commitment to helping others.

What mistakes have you made?

I would say a lack of follow up, occasional procrastination, and not working when I don't feel like it. I learned the hard way that you need to nurture and work a little bit on your business everyday.

In your opinion, what does it really take to achieve your level of success?

One needs a total commitment to WORK! A daily positive attitude in spite of circumstances.

What are your top sales tips?

Never use high-pressure sales techniques. Always ask for referrals whether it is for your product or for your business opportunity. Also, I believe in always providing excellent customer service, no hype. Act like you, not like someone else! Build long-term relationships with your customers—it's not always about the sale!

What are your top recruiting tips? What helps you recruit?

Timely follow up is crucial. Expect they will want to say "yes" and always agree with your prospect, no matter what their objection. It certainly helps that I always look like a Jewelry Lady when I'm out. I believe in always telling the truth, talking with everyone I meet, and making sure that I don't prejudge them whether they may be interested or not.

What have you earned at the company (trips, cars, prizes, etc.)

I've earned/won jewelry (we don't have a car program, but hey, my car has been paid for with my jewelry income!). I have also earned many trips on which my husband has also been able to join me. For example, we've been to Toronto, Canada; Orlando, FL; Dallas, TX, and three cruises—the latest being an eight-day Mexican Riviera cruise in May 2005, compliments of Premier Designs!

What words of advice can you give to a consultant who really wants to grow their business?

Go to your local training and national rallies.

What do you want to achieve next?

The next level of leadership for me in Premier Designs would be a natural progression from 2-Diamond Designer, my current level, to 3-Diamond Designer.

What do you enjoy most: Recruiting or sales? Why?

I enjoy sponsoring—we do not call it "recruiting" in Premier Designs—plus helping others to achieve *their* goals for their family!

How many parties should you hold each week?

I think one should hold one to two a week to keep their business momentum. However, let me add that it is not about what I think—each person needs to set goals that will work best for them and their family—not what someone else expects of them. The key is, if one sets their goal at holding one show per week, and they meet their goal, they are successful in their business.

What about bookings? How do you get bookings?

Be excited about what you have to offer, and always ask everyone! If I leave a show with zero bookings, then that means I have some "homework" to do!

How about your hostess? How do you coach her?

Hostess coaching is imperative to leading and to growing a successful business! I set the hostess coaching appointment at the same time when they have booked their show. I go to her home and at the same time, I share our marketing plan.

How do you develop leads for your business?

My leads come from home shows, networking, word-of-mouth referrals, and wearing my jewelry when I am out.

What is your primary marketing method?

Referrals and word-of-mouth work best for me.

What advice can you give on joining local leads and business groups?

I think they can be a great idea and help to increase one's network. One needs to be careful not to spend all their time going to leads groups and not focusing on keeping "the main thing" the main thing—meaning working their business in the areas of sales and sponsoring.

What tips can you give about advertising? Has it worked for you?

Save the advertising dollars—use word of mouth, and ask for referrals!

Give some tips about inventory…does a new consultant need a lot?

No. Don't buy out the farm! With our company, we don't have inventory—we have samples! It is always better to have a sample-based business rather than an inventory-based business because inventory is not tax deductible, but samples are tax deductible.

What is your advice for recruiting and building a strong team? How do you manage them?

Build relationships with the people on your team. Ask them what their goals are—have them write them down. Ask them in what areas do they need your help or expertise. Have them go to a few of your shows for on-the-job training. Encourage them to practice their presentation with you in plenty of time before they have their first show. Schedule group fun times. Remember their birthdays! Help them to become "independent" consultants and not "dependent" consultants—don't do everything for them, or they will never grow their own business.

What are your most important learning experiences?

First, *never, never* give up. Second, never prejudge someone's interest level. And, finally, sometimes one must fail in order to succeed.

Tips about motivation…how have you kept yourself motivated in order to rise to your professional level of success?

I keep my goals in front of me every day and review how I am doing toward working to meet those goals.

What are your top tips for a fun, profitable party?

Laugh at yourself—see humor in every situation! If people are having fun, they will want to book a show with you. Always remember guests' names. Pay sincere compliments to your guests. The Bible says "a merry heart does good like a medicine."

What advice can you offer to someone looking for a direct sales company to join?

Talk to others who currently are with and who used to be with that company. Do some internet research. Get the facts for yourself—don't take someone else's word for it. Determine if they are a people-oriented company or a profit-oriented company. Steer clear of those companies who give you a high-pressure sales pitch or who try to attach themselves to you like a bumper sticker to a car, chasing you down the road at every turn.

Any final tips or ideas?

Never say something negative about another company, even if it is true!

☙

Drop a stake in the ground. Believe in your business and yourself 100% and then be persistent. If you dig your stake in the ground far enough, it won't fly away at the first rough weather. *R.G., AZ*

NOTES:

End Note

Contratulations! By finishing this book, you've taken one more important step toward your own success. Prior to reading this book, you may already have some systems that work for you and some success to propel you forward. However, we bet you've learned a thing or two that you may be considering implementing into your own business plan.

These participating sellers are the entrepreneurs you can refer back to time and again whenever you have doubts or hear about how direct sales is a "tough business." Whenever you have a bad day and think maybe you should just sell your kit on ebay and get a job, remember these sellers who like you, surely had those days too. The naysayers in life are plentiful; mentors are harder to find.

We've counseled and consulted with direct sales professionals on many levels for a few years now. We have heard the stories of defeat, the less-than-excited attitudes and the fear of just doing what needed to be done. We also know that when an idea clicks, it's amazing. All of a sudden you can see possibilities and have a new drive to continue. Hopefully this book has helped you get a few "light bulb clicks" of your own to inspire you to keep on trying.

As you read through the interviews, you likely saw some of the same things being said time and again. There is a reason that these sellers repeat the same phrases…they work. The number one word of advice would be to have perseverance. Don't give up! Also, having patience is a very important advice point we heard several times. Your success will not happen overnight. "Shopping around" to find a sponsor that will help you grow and with whom you have great communication is another wonderful tip. Signing up with the first person who offers you the opportunity may be convenient, but if you really want to grow your business, find someone who can help you along until you feel strong enough to fly solo.

Some sellers chanted "recruit, recruit, recruit" when asked how to really build a successful direct sales business. They know the power sponsoring has on their bank balance, but they also know it's the way to really help others. It's the personal touch that some of the sellers incited as the reason to work in direct sales. The ability to really know your customer and to help your customer feel special is enviable in these days of big box retailers.

Finally, their honesty about how to stay motivated what mistakes they've made and what their weak spots are is refreshing and probably just as helpful as the positive ideas they've shared. Knowing a top seller, someone you may want to emulate, has stumbled like you really shines a light on the fact that it isn't a magic act they've done. They've worked hard, made mistakes, experienced success and it all came by putting one foot in front of the other day after day.

One thing is clear; these sellers are people just like you and me. They have come to this stage in their careers after many months, years, even decades, to refine a well-oiled machine. It's their well-oiled machine. And that is what is most enviable of all. They built it brick by brick, so to speak, with their own sweat and tears.

Good luck, stay positive and keep this book within eyesight for those days when nothing you do seems good enough. This book has given you a glimpse into the world of what being a successful top seller is like and how you can walk down the path to become one too!

&

Annual Business Plan

Personal Income Goal: $75,000 net income
Personal Team Goal: Add 45+ recruits

Overview Goal Statement:

This is my year to really succeed at becoming a mega-recruiter and build my team. I will continue to book parties, sell, and recruit while refining my skills and having even more fun. I will work to mentor my team members to grow themselves. I will read at least four motivational books and listen to one full tape program. I will write and define my Monthly Business Focus and commit to following my monthly and weekly goals.

I will work toward the goal of hiring a part-time assistant to help with marketing and administrative duties. I will work toward developing more internet business and commit to doing monthly sales promotions on my website. I will write and send quarterly newsletters and develop a local referral guide for my customers. I will develop a lead-generating system and follow-up system that I will stick with. I will also begin to see more re-orders as I commit to follow up with past customers with monthly phone calls and/or emails. I will commit to doing a monthly sales promotion.

I will see my team develop as a strong force as I commit to recruiting at least one to two people per week. I will recruit from parties and past customers. I will work with new recruits to teach them patience and enthusiasm and show them the possibilities available with this company. I will dedicate my efforts to helping them get started and keep moving forward depending upon their goals. I will work to reduce drop outs by keeping in touch and providing personal service to my team members. My team members will feel a part of a special family via my efforts.

(Example: First six months of business plan)

January

Send *Happy New Year* notes/promotion to all past customers, hostesses, etc.
Develop my Monthly Business Focus (MBF) and define my weekly duties.
Hold four parties
Book future four parties
Recruit four people
Work to stay focused on my goals

February

Send *Valentine's Day* promotions on first of the month
Refine my MBF: Define my weeks
Hold six parties
Book future four parties
Recruit four people
Hold monthly team meeting
Develop monthly sales contest for my team:
   Encourage bookings and recruiting
Develop local referral booklet: Get participation from local sellers

March

Send *End of Winter Sale* promotion and newsletter
Refine my MBF: Define my weeks
   Focus on developing and encouraging my team
Hold six parties
Book future six parties
Recruit five people
Hold team meeting: Give team sales awards/gifts

April

Send *Happy Spring* promotion and newsletter
Refine my MBF: Define my weeks:
   Focusing on developing my name/business in the community
Hold six parties

Book future six parties
Recruit six people
Recruiting Focus:
>Hold team meeting for training, awards, support, etc.
>Keep in touch with each team member with calls/emails

Join local business group

May

Send *Pre-Summer Specials* promotion and newsletter
Refine my MBF: Define my weeks:
>Strong focus on recruiting

Hold six parties
Book future six parties
Recruit eight people
Hold team meeting: Awards, etc.
Attend local business group meeting
Identify and develop my personal recruiting system
>Start planning for July-December recruiting goals

June

Send *Summer Specials* promotion and newsletter
Refine my MBF: Define my weeks:
>Strong focus on recruiting and managing

Hold six parties
Book future six parties
Recruit eight people
Hold team meeting: Awards, etc.
Attend local business group meeting
Contact any possible recruits from January/February interest file

Excerpts included in this book:

Your Dream Day: A Mini-Plan for Success
Excerpt from the Direct Seller's Boot Camp

Marketing Tips
Excerpt from PUMP News Guides

Have Shyness, Will Succeed
Excerpt from the Direct Seller Guide: Get Booked Solid!

Working From Home: No License for Laundry
Excerpt from PUMP News Guides

What's Your Plan?
Excerpt from PUMP News Guides

Create a Referral Rainfall!
Excerpt from the Direct Sales Business Blaster

For more information about these items, visit www.isellmoretoday.com

Additional resources available from MOEHR & ASSOCIATES

Visit www.isellmoretoday.com for more information.

Direct Seller Guide: Get Booked Solid!

A powerful resource plan for booking a solid calendar of sales events. If you find yourself wondering "*How can I get more bookings?*" this program is your answer. An easy-to-use and inexpensive program you can quickly implement in your marketing efforts.

PUMP Member News Guides

Written specifically for the direct sales professional, PUMP is a quarterly newsletter packed full of marketing tips for sales, recruiting, service and business growth. It even includes a different interview with a top seller in each issue!

Direct Sales Business Blaster

A straight-forward booklet of advice and ideas for developing and growing a strong direct sales downline. No fluff, no banter, just a solid resource for developing your most important asset—your team.

Direct Seller Boot Camp

Our most intense and comprehensive program. The Boot Camp includes all items listed above plus our unique 30-Days to Success Calendar filled with task-a-day items to get your business from zero to $$$$ in just 30 days.

Karen Moehr started Moehr & Associates in Portland, Oregon in 1996. It began as a general marketing assistance company with an emphasis on helping small or home-based business. Her focus changed when she attended a home sales party in 2003. She expressed a slight interest in the company and its products and the rep called her six times in the following few days to try to sign her as a new recruit. After facing such pressure, she decided it wasn't the opportunity for her.

This unfortunate experience lead her to wonder about the industry. After talking with a friend who was in working in direct sales and facing the problem of how to grow her business, she quickly realized there was a need for dedicated marketing assistance to help direct sales professionals grow their business. Her own experience in addition to her friend's experience gave her the impetus to create the *Direct Seller Guide: Get Booked Solid!*, a publication geared toward helping reps get bookings for sales parties.

Its popularity spurred the creation of the *PUMP News Guide*, a quarterly newsletter for direct sales professionals and then the development of the *Direct Seller Boot Camp* and *Direct Sales Business Blaster*. Each publication has its own focus and can assist the sales professional with marketing, growth, service, referrals, bookings, and recruiting.

Karen earned a B.A. in Communications and Psychology; two disciplines that work well with her personal style and commitment to helping people grow their businesses. Her personalized consulting service is offered to purchasers of her online publications. She enjoys writing and producing marketing publications but working one-on-one with a confused or frustrated seller is her real passion. She enjoys helping people identify new marketing avenues for their business and being a part of helping them create their own success.

Moehr & Associates has provided marketing and corporate communications services to small and medium-sized business from home-based sole proprietors to national, multi-state corporations. Karen moved her business to Tucson, Arizona in late 2004 where she continues to write and consult with small business professionals in various industries.